The Essence of Nectar

Yeshe Tsöndru

Translated by
Geshe Lobsang Tharchin
with
Benjamin & Deborah Alterman

LIBRARY OF TIBETAN WORKS AND ARCHIVES

ISBN: 81-85102-02-3

Published by the Library of Tibetan Works and Archives, Dharamsala, H.P., India, and printed at Indraprastha Press (CBT), 4 Bahadur Shah Zafar Marg, New Delhi-110002 ·

Publisher's Note

We are happy to bring out this revised edition of *The Essence of Nectar* by Yeshe Tsondru, ably rendered into English by Geshe Lobsang Tharchin with Benjamin and Deborah Alterman, as a continuation of our programme of publishing translations of original Tibetan texts for the benefit of interested readers.

Gyatsho Tshering
Director
Library of Tibetan Works & Archives

November 1994

Contents

Foreword

The Essence of Nectar is a compendium of the extensive teachings which are presented in such texts as the *Lam Rim Chen Mo* of Je Tsong Ka Pa. It sets forth the complete path to Buddhahood in stages to be practised in sequence by one who wishes to follow this path.

The lineage of these teachings originated with Buddha Shakyamuni and was passed down through an unbroken succession of Indian masters to the great pandit Atisa who, after coming to Tibet, composed the *Bodhipathapradipam* which has served as the prototype for all subsequent Lam Rim texts. From Atisa, the lineage was passed down through an unbroken succession of Tibetan masters to Je Tsongkhapa and has continued unbroken to the present.

The Essence of Nectar was composed by a holder of this lineage, an incarnation of Thegchen Tulku named Yeshe Tsondru of Sera Me College, Kong Po house (Ser-smad kong-po theg-chen sprul-sku ye-shes brtson-'grus).

Geshe Lobsang Tharchin of Sera Me College, Gyal Rong house (Ser-smad rgyal-rong dge-bshes blo-bzang mthar-phyin) graduated with a Geshe Lharampa degree from Sera Me Monastic College and then from Gyu Me Tantric College in Lhasa. He received the lineage of the Lam Rim teachings along with extensive oral tradition explanation from Kyab Je Pabong Kha Rinpoche—Root Guru of Kyab Je Trijang Rinpoche; from Kyab Je Trijang Rinpoche—Junior Tutor to His Holiness the Fourteenth Dalai Lama; from His Holiness the Fourteenth Dalai Lama; and from Tre Hor Kyor Pon Rinpoche, as well as from many other renowned teachers in this lineage.

During the autumn and winter of 1976-77, Geshe Tharchin taught this text to a group of his students at Rashi Gempil Ling in Freewood Acres, New Jersey. Benjamin and Deborah Alterman prepared the present written translation from the Tibetan text, according to Geshe Tharchin's oral translation and explanation.

Geshe Tharchin's commentary and instructions for practising this text appear in the notes. Explanations of terms and enumerations appear in the glossary. Words within square brackets are the author's own words which appeared in small print in the Tibetan text. Words in parenthesis are the translators' insertions.

Special thanks are due to India Trinley for editing the manuscript and her many suggestions, to Sherpa Tulku for his discerning comments, and to the students in Geshe Tharchin's class.

This translation was made with the hope of benefitting those who wish to learn the practices taught by the Buddha.

Preliminary Practices

The essence of nectar—the supreme Dharma, the way to practise profound instructions on the stages of the Bodhi path as set forth in verse is herein contained.[1]

I make obeisance and go for refuge to the illustrious, peerless spiritual masters, my Root Gurus together with the lineage gurus, each being the combination of all the victorious ones of the three times. May I be cared for by them without interruption in this and all my successive lives.[2]

Herein, by means of verse, I will briefly explain the way for fortunate disciples to practise the profound instructions on the stages of the Bodhi path.

The Stage of Going for Refuge[3]

Before me amid an ocean-like cloud of marvellous offerings, atop a majestic jewelled throne supported by eight snow lions, on discs of lotus, the sun, and the full moon, the Conqueror—Lord of Sages, indistinguishable from my Root Guru, a master Teacher of the unerring path, sits radiantly in the centre of a network of light rays.

With grandeur like the summit of golden Mount Meru, he wears the three (saffron) robes of a monk and glows with the magnificent marks of perfection. His right hand presses the earth; his left hand, placed in the gesture of meditation, holds an alms bowl filled with nectar. His form is an embodiment of majestic splendor upon which I can never gaze enough.

Just as the multitude of stars surround the moon, so all the spiritual masters of the three lineages sit encircling this supreme, peerless teacher. Around these direct and lineage gurus is the assembly of Tantric deities, Buddhas of the ten directions, spiritual sons, hearkeners, solitary victors, celestials, and Dharma protectors.

On elegant tables to the right and left of each individual are arranged the volumes of authoritative teachings which have come from each one. The syllables (of these works) emit their own melodious sounds of Dharma.

From the bodily parts of every object of refuge luminous beams radiate in ten directions, and from the end of each of these rays countless emanations go forth and ripen sentient beings.

Looking upon me with compassion, (my Root Guru) says, "Fortunate son, if you wish for liberation from the suffering of cyclic existence, I shall guide you." His smiling countenance comforts and delights me.

Surrounding me are all sentient beings, including my parents, delirious with sufferings of the six types of beings. Looking here and there, searching for refuge, they weep and cry out pathetically.

Alas, from beginningless time until now, I have wandered throughout the six realms, always tormented by numerous sufferings; never have I found a moment free of them.

Now I have a rare opportunity, a life with leisure and endowments, as well as acquaintance with the supreme teachings and a master teacher. But it is so difficult to dispel the mental afflictions to which I have been subject from beginningless time that I despair of reaching a state of permanent safety.

There is no assurance that death will not come today, nor can I choose my next place of rebirth. If I fall into the abyss of the unfortunate realms, will that suffering be bearable for even an instant?

Though once in a great while I obtain high rebirth as a god or man, still I am continually oppressed by innumerable sufferings, including birth, sickness, aging, and death, and since I shall again fall into the unfortunate realms, what security is there in high rebirths?

I have obtained a life of leisure and endowments, am cared for by a supreme spiritual guide who teaches the path, and know both the benefits of transcendence and the faults of cyclic existence. At this time I must quickly free myself from dreadful cyclic existence.

To free myself alone is insufficient, however, because each and every sentient being who wanders throughout cyclic existence has (previously) been my parent. I must therefore free them from cyclic existence as well.

There is no protection or refuge other than the Three Jewels which can liberate me and every being from the vast ocean of limitless cyclic existence.

Therefore:

> I and all sentient beings,
> Equal (in number to the extent of) space
> For however long it takes until our attainment of Bodhi,
> Go for refuge to the direct and lineage gurus,
> Go for refuge to the master teachers, the Buddhas,
> Go for refuge to the supreme Dharma, the teachings and realizations,
> Go for refuge to the exalted assembly, the Sangha.
> *(Recite this verse three, seven, or numerous times.)*

When we take refuge in this way, the objects of refuge are pleased, and from their bodies flows a stream of ambrosia, which completely eliminates from myself and every sentient being the non-virtues, obstructions, sickness, evil spirits, and other conditions unfavorable to life. In particular, it cleanses all our erroneous conduct regarding the Three Jewels. Our lifespan, collection of merit, (acquaintance with) teachings, realizations, and virtuous qualities greatly increase. I and all other sentient beings come under the protection of the Three Jewels.

Generation of the Bodhi Mind

I am bound in the prison of cyclic existence by the chains of my deeds and mental afflictions. Just as I am tormented, so are all miserable sentient beings who again and again have been my mother and nurtured me with kindness.

The responsibility to liberate these beings has fallen on me, but at a time like this when there is little or no way of knowing where I myself shall go (after death), I have no hope of liberating others.

Even attainment of the two types of arhatship is not completely beneficial for me and is only partially beneficial for others. Therefore, in order to be of ultimate benefit to myself and others, I must definitely achieve the state of the victorious ones.

If I attain this supreme state, my own encumbrances will come to an end and all virtuous qualities, without exception, will be achieved; effortlessly, I shall be able to help my mothers—the sentient beings who pervade all space.

Therefore, I must quickly attain perfect Buddhahood, and to that end, without becoming discouraged, I shall follow step by step the great practices of (Bodhisattva) conduct—generosity and so forth.

By the force of the supreme Bodhi mind that I have generated in this way, all the gurus, victorious ones, and spiritual sons are extremely pleased. From the body of the Lord of Sages, a duplicate (appears) which dissolves into me, purifying me of all non-virtue and obstructions. I am transformed into the body of the Lord of Sages from which beams of light radiate in ten directions, cleansing impure places and their inhabitants of faults (so that they) become thoroughly pure.

The Four Immeasurables

Oh, even though all sentient beings have been born countless times as each other's parents, without knowing this they have accumulated bad deeds through attachment and hatred; thus, they experience only suffering. How wonderful it would be if, separated from that attachment and hatred, they would now abide in a state of equanimity.

> May they abide (in equanimity).
> I must bring this about.
> Please bestow inspiring strength
> So that I may be able to do this.

Oh, even though all sentient beings wish only for continuous happiness, not knowing that the cause of happiness is virtue or, even when knowing this, being unable to practise virtue, they lack happiness. How wonderful it would be if they were now to possess happiness and the cause of happiness.

> May they possess (happiness and its cause).
> I must bring this about.
> Please bestow inspiring strength
> So that I may be able to do this.

Oh, even though all sentient beings never wish for any suffering, because of their extreme ignorance which reverses what should be adopted and what should be renounced, they always participate in erroneous non-virtuous deeds; thus, they are tormented by suffering. How wonderful it would be if they were now separated from suffering and the cause of suffering.

> May they be separated (from suffering and its cause).
> I must bring this about.
> Please bestow inspiring strength
> So that I may be able to do this.

Oh, after all sentient beings have become separated from the suffering and causes of cyclic existence and particularly of unfortunate rebirths, how wonderful it would be if gradually they could attain the bliss of high rebirths and definite goodness, never to be separated from supreme, uncontaminated bliss.

> May they never be separated (from that supreme bliss).
> I must bring this about.
> Please bestow inspiring strength
> So that I may be able to do this.

The Special Development of the Bodhi Mind

In order to liberate all beings equal (in number to the extent of) space, I must quickly attain Buddhahood. To this end, I shall practise the profound instructions on the stages of the bodhi path.

Visualization of the Field of the Accumulation of Merit

> In order to easily enter (this practice), it has been stated that it is sufficient to merely recall, at this point, the objects of refuge which were previously (visualized) and not yet dissolved.
>
> It has been stated that, at this time, you should invoke (the objects of refuge) and offer ablution to them in the following way:

Invoking the Refuge Objects and Offering Ablution

All you assembled direct and lineage gurus, Tantric deities, Buddhas, Bodhisattvas, hearkeners, solitary victors, heroes, celestials, and Dharma protectors, who dwell in (pure) realms pervading space, each and every one of you, out of compassion, please give me your attention.

For countless eons you have not forgotten your vows to develop the supreme bodhi mind for our benefit. Like the lord of birds (appearing) from the heavens, by the force of supernormal manifestation, out of compassion, please come here.[4]

Thus the invocation is made.

In a fragrantly scented bath chamber with a brightly shining floor of crystal, beautiful pillars of glittering jewels, and a canopy of glowing pearls, I offer ablution (to the objects of refuge) with pure divine water, just as the gods offered ablution to (Buddha Shakyamuni) at the time of his birth.

Although the (perfect) body, speech and mind of the victorious ones are not subject to mental afflictions, in order to wash away the defilements from the body, speech and mind of all sentient beings, I offer this water for ablution to the victorious ones. May the body, speech and mind of sentient beings thereby be cleansed.

Using numerous jewelled urns overflowing with pleasantly scented water—the music of many musicians (playing)—I offer ablution to the ones gone thus and all their spiritual sons.

This excellent water, most glorious, is the unsurpassable water of great compassion; it is the inspiring water of wisdom. Please grant the accomplishment of my wishes.

Now I dry the bodies (of these objects of refuge) with an incomparable towel, (immaculately) clean and infused with fragrant perfumes.
OM HUM TRAM HRIH AH KAYA VISHO-DHANA-YE SVA-HA.

In order to purify my mind, I offer exquisite clothes which are as bright and beautiful as the variegated rainbow and, when touched, are causes of bliss. (Thus) may I be adorned with the clothing of enduring patience.

Because they possess natural adornment, the major and minor marks of perfection, I cannot adorn the victorious ones further. Even so, by my offering fine, jewelled ornaments (to them), may all sentient beings attain bodies bearing the marks of perfection.

I offer surroundings of love, (hung) with fluttering banners, and a canopy of concentration, bright with the luminescence of courage—necessities which are suitable, useful and excellent. May (all) beings attain pure wisdom.

Please, O Conqueror, out of compassion for myself and all sentient beings and by the force of your supernormal power, remain here while I make these offerings.

Thus (the ceremony of ablution) is performed.

The way to practise the seven limbs which comprise the main points of collecting (merit) and purifying (non-virtue and obstructions) follows:

The Seven-limbed Practice

I make obeisance to the Guru, Lord of Sages, who is in this world the manifestation of the three secrets, and who said, "During times of strife, I shall guide all beings who have not been tamed by the many previous Buddhas."

I make obeisance to the direct and lineage gurus, who, by their consummately skilful means of instruction on the vast, profound Sutras and Tantras, lead me from the immensity of misery, the ocean of cyclic existence in which I am drowning, to the stairway of the three precious bodies.

I make obeisance to the assembled Deities of the four classes of Tantra, who grant in a instant the state of unification, which is difficult to attain even if one strenuously practicses for many eons.[5]

I make obeisance to all the Buddhas, the master teachers, who, by the force of their acquaintance for countless eons with the two accumulations, have eliminated all faults and achieved every virtuous quality and who act (on behalf of sentient beings) spontaneously and continuously.

I make obeisance to the supreme Dharma—the teachings and realizations—which, if relied upon, purifies every fault and fully gives all excellence of high rebirths and definite goodness.

I make obeisance to the supreme spiritual sons of the victorious ones, who never consider their own happiness even in their dreams. With great courage, disinterested in their own bodies and lives, they always strive for the happiness of others.

I make obeisance to the exalted ones who are hearkeners and solitary victors. Having seen all the realms of cyclic existence as a fiery pit, they relied upon the vehicle of the three trainings. Thus, they set out for and reached the city of liberation.

I make obeisance to the heroes and celestials in the twenty-four supreme sacred places, who, out of loving concern at all times for practitioners, emanate in manifestations like those depicted in religious dramas.

I make obeisance to the Dharma protectors, who have vowed to smash into dust the hosts of evil spirits and to satisfy every wish of those who properly practise the supreme Dharma.

In brief, (visualizing) manifestations of my body equal in number to the planets and pure realms and chanting an ocean of praise to the virtuous qualities (of the objects of refuge), with indestructible faith and great respect, I make obeisance to all those who are worthy of veneration.

Joyfully, without reluctance or attachment, I offer all of this in order to please (the objects of refuge):[6]

—elegant, capacious vessels (made of) precious materials filled with a libation, the ambrosia of immortality

—cool, spring-fed pools of water possessing eight qualities, (offered for bathing) the feet, (each pool located along) the banks of a lake adorned with delightful lotuses

—fields covered with many lovely flowers such as water lily, moon-flower and lotus

—the air filled with clouds of fragrant incense made from fine medicinal ingredients

—the bright, attractive glow of candles and lamps as well as the light from jewels, the sun and the moon

—gently undulating waves of cool, perfumed water infused with camphor and sandal

—a banquet of the invigorating foods of gods and men enhanced with hundreds of colours, tastes, and aromas

—the varied music of strings, woodwinds, cymbals and drums resonating throughout the three levels (of earth)

—exquisite forms; superb smells, tastes and pleasing sounds; an infinite variety of alluring tactile sensations

—the seven supreme treasures of a ruler of men

—(natural) formations of the eight auspicious signs covering the ground

—verdant forests, enchanting flowers, lakes, oceans and so forth

—whatever offerings there are without owner as well as all the possessions and the physical forms of myself and others

—whatever accumulation of virtue I have gathered from having heard, contemplated and meditated upon the ocean of oral instructions (that explain) Buddha's teachings of Sutra and Tantra.

These marvellous offerings—clouds of sublime offerings vividly arising from the force (of my concentration)—I extend to all fields of the accumulation of merit.

I present this ocean-like cloud of many types of offerings produced by my faith, intention and concentration (to you, O objects of refuge). Out of your great compassion, please accept them; then let the accomplishment of all desirable goals fall (like) rain on me and every sentient being.[7]

At this point, the Confession of Moral Downfalls and the like may be done or not, according to one's wish. Then:

From my heart I confess and (promise to) refrain from every natural and proscribed non-virtuous deed of the three doors which I have committed previously or urged (others) to commit, (since these deeds are) the sole cause of all the immeasurable sufferings.[8]

With great reverence and sincerity, I rejoice in the excellent activities—past, present and future—of the supreme direct and lineage gurus, the innumerable victorious ones, and the spiritual sons.[9]

Since we have fallen off the steep cliff of cyclic existence into the depths of misfortune and are oppressed by the thick pitch-darkness of suffering, please show the light of Dharma, the path to liberation, to myself and all beings who know not what to do.[10]

With your skilful means and great compassion for us disciples who pervade all space, please remain as our protector in whatever physical manifestation will tame us until every being has reached supreme bodhi.[11]

I dedicate whatever virtue has been accumulated through actions such as these to the purpose of quickly attaining unsurpassable bodhi, so that I may place on the path to everlasting bliss all these mother sentient beings who have become weary on the road of cyclic existence.[12]

At this point make a mandala offering. Then, according to the oral instructions make requests in the following way:[13]

Requests

Glorious, precious Root Guru sitting on a lotus and moon above my head, out of your great kindness take care of me and grant the attainment of (your perfect) body, speech, and mind.[14]

You who are in the centre of the one thousand world leaders of this fortunate eon, you who have especially great compassion for the beings in this time of strife, O supreme spiritual master—Lord of Sages—Holder of the Vajra, please bestow inspiring strength on the continuum of my mind.

All you assembled spiritual masters (in the lineage that) bestows the inspiring strength of (Tantric) practice, who lead to the State of Unification in one lifetime the fortunate disciples who rely upon the practices of great Tantric deities, please bestow inspiring strength on the continuum of my mind.

All you assembled spiritual masters in the lineage of vast (Bodhisattva) conduct, who, moved by great compassion, teach sentient beings the main points of the extensive paths (of Bodhi mind)—the hidden meaning of the Transcendental Wisdom (Sutras), please bestow inspiring strength on the continuum of my mind.

All you assembled spiritual masters in the lineage of the profound view, who place ignorant beings deludedly wandering (in cyclic existence) securely onto the profound path of peace which is free from the illusion (of self-existence), please bestow inspiring strength on the continuum of my mind.

All you assembled spiritual masters in the Ka-dam lineage, who hold the vast and profound methods of teaching and spread the doctrine of the supreme vehicle in the Land of Snow, please bestow inspiring strength on the continuum of my mind.

All you assembled spiritual masters in the Ga-dan Ka-dam lineage, who give excellent instruction on combining all the Sutras, Tantras, and commentaries into a (graduated) path by which a person can reach bodhi, please bestow inspiring strength on the continuum of my mind.

All you beneficent root gurus, you who are the great compassion of the innumerable victorious ones appearing in the form of supreme spiritual guides, master teachers of the path, please bestow inspiring strength on the continuum of my mind.

Now recite the "Yon-tan zhi-gyur-ma", or if you wish to do something more extensive, (continue as follows:)[15]

All you supreme spiritual masters who show the unerring path, please bestow inspiring strength so that I may never develop (for even) an instant the mistaken thought (that you are) ordinary (beings). May I (always) perceive what you do as excellent, and by remembering your kindness, practise according to your words.[16]

Please bestow inspiring strength so that I quickly overcome my indolence and carelessness, states of mind that waste (this) good foundation of leisure and endowments, making it meaningless. May I take full advantage of (this life's) great meaning from heartfelt remembrance (of its) rarity and purpose.

Please bestow inspiring strength so that I cease grasping (at this life as something) enduring, which is certain to last for a hundred years, even though I see that (the time of) death is without certainty. From (the depths of my) heart may I remember the condition of life—that it will end soon and that the time of death is indefinite.

Please bestow inspiring strength so that I root out from my thoughts and actions even the slightest indifference towards the un-bearable abyss of the three (unfortunate realms). May I develop great fear by merely recalling what I have seen and heard of the conditions of unfortunate rebirths.

Please bestow inspiring strength so that I become completely free from the ruinous state of mind of not seeking salvation even though I see the dangers (of cyclic existence). May I take heartfelt refuge in the Three Supreme Jewels, the only infallible salvation.

Please bestow inspiring strength so that I put an end to my deluded state of mind which lacks conviction, even though I have heard and seen hundreds of cases of deeds and results. May I gain genuine conviction about the way in which black and white deeds have results.[17]

Please bestow inspiring strength so that I become free from the state of mind in which I perceive all the places, forms, and pleasures of cyclic existence as happiness and yearn for them. May I fervently generate a desire for liberation by realizing that the three places of existence are like a fiery pit.

Please bestow inspiring strength so that I banish my enemy, grasping at self-existence, which has bound me to this prison of cyclic existence from beginningless time. May I become skilled in the practice of the three trainings, the complete and unerring path to liberation.

Please bestow inspiring strength so that I never develop the inferior state of mind of neglecting sentient beings and striving for the bliss of solitary peace. May I develop very quickly the supreme attitude of taking responsibility for others' welfare.

Please bestow inspiring strength so that I expel this chronic disease of self-cherishing, the sole cause of all the encumbrances of cyclic existence and solitary transcendence. May I become imbued (with the attitude of) cherishing others, the only door to all good things for myself and other beings.

Please bestow inspiring strength so that I never lack, even for an instant, courage to enter the ocean-like activities of the spiritual sons. May I practise the conduct of the six perfections as (exemplified) in the life histories of the courageous ones who abide in the (Bodhisattva) stages.

Please bestow inspiring strength so that I pacify all obfuscations— dullness, agitation, and their symptoms, the main obstacles to the accomplishment of perfect deep concentration. May I develop effortless concentration which controls at will my entire mental focus.

Please bestow inspiring strength so that I never develop the perverted views of eternalism and nihilism, which are contrary to the actual meaning of the Victorious One's teachings. May I soon perceive without illusion the fundamental true nature (by realizing that) voidness and appearance are complementary.[18]

Please bestow inspiring strength so that I may be free from the state of mind in which I pretend to seek out the quick path (of Tantra, while actually I am) afraid to engage in the powerful practices. May I enter the great secret vehicle with the intention of liberating all beings more quickly.

Please bestow inspiring strength so that I purify all my defilements—erroneous deeds and moral downfalls which transgress the major and minor rules that I promised (to keep) at the time of empowerment. By seeing that my vows and adherence are the basis of the path, may I cherish and protect them just as I do my life.[19]

Please bestow inspiring strength so that I become free from the fears of ordinary birth, death and the intermediate state, which join me to suffering for as long as I am in cyclic existence. May I master the two stages (of Tantra) in which the world and its inhabitants appear as emanations of the three vajra bodies.[20]

Please bestow inspiring strength so that I dispel, in the meantime, all outer and inner hindrances with their symptoms, the obstacles for practising the noble path. May I spontaneously and effortlessly obtain all favorable conditions and auspiciousness.

In all my successive lives, may I obtain a foundation of leisure and endowments and meet with spiritual guides like those who have shown me the path. By hearing, contemplating and meditating, may I quickly pass through the levels and paths,[21] attain omniscience, and liberate all beings.

*Having made these requests, proceed according to oral instructions with the visualizations for requesting inspiring strength in **Opening the Door to the Supreme Path**. Then, according to your wish, you may either merge with the Field of the Accumulation of Merit, as (instructed in) **De-lam**, or not, as (instructed in) **Jam-pal zhal-lung**.*

Teachings in Common with a Person of Small Scope

The Stages of the Path

The Advantages of Devotion to a Spiritual Guide

The advantages of proper devotion by thought and action to a virtuous spiritual guide who shows the complete and unerring supreme bodhi path are inconceivable, because (the Buddha) said that the great state of unification, which is extremely difficult to attain even by diligent practice for countless ocean-like eons, is easily achieved in one short life during this time of degeneration if one relies upon the power of a spiritual master.

It is said that when one devotes himself properly to a supreme spiritual guide, he will soon be free from cyclic existence, and all the victorious ones will rejoice from the depths of their hearts and minds, as do mothers when they see their children benefitted.

(The Buddha) said that when a disciple is properly devoted to a spiritual master, all the victorious ones gladly enter into the body of that spiritual master, even though not invoked; then, accepting the accumulated offerings, the victorious ones bestow inspiring strength upon the disciple's mental continuum.

At that time inspiring strength from all the Buddhas enters through the opening of one's faithful mind; by its force, the hosts of evil spirits and mental afflictions can cause no harm and realizations of the stages and paths immediately develop and increase.

If one always reverently relies upon a spiritual master, then all mental afflictions and erroneous activities will end of their own accord, and one's virtuous faculties will naturally increase. One will therefore obtain extensive happiness in this and future lives.

Since results accord with their cause,[22] if one has pleased (one's) Guru in this life, then in all successive lives he will meet with a virtuous spiritual guide and hear the complete unerring supreme Dharma.

In brief, while devoting oneself to a spiritual guide, one will find freedom from the states of no leisure and obtain the fortunate birth of a god or man. Ultimately all one's suffering in cyclic existence will come to an end, and one will attain the sublime state of definite goodness.

The Disadvantages of Lacking Devotion (to a Spiritual Guide)

Just as the advantages of proper devotion to a spiritual guide are inconceivable, likewise the disadvantages of a lack of devotion or a breach of devotion are also inconceivable.

(The Buddha) said that because all virtuous spiritual guides are the deeds of the victorious ones appearing as one's spiritual master, being disrespectful to them is (the same as) being disrespectful to all the victorious ones. What (could possibly bring) a heavier matured result than that?

It is stated in the *Kalacakra Tantra* that for however many moments one develops anger towards (one's) spiritual master, the virtue accumulated during that many eons is destroyed, and for as many eons as the number of those moments, one will be born in hell.

(The Buddha) said that if one who has committed atrocities such as the five heinous deeds relies upon Tantra, one can attain even the supreme (state of unification) in that very life. But one who despises (one's) spiritual master from the depths of one's heart cannot succeed in developing any attainments whatsoever, even if one has practiced for eons.

It is explained in the Tantras that if a person purposely humiliates the spiritual guide who shows (one) the path, then even if he makes an effort to abandon sleep, unquiet, and lethargy—the best way to strive for Tantric goals—it is like striving (for a rebirth in) hell.

If one lacks respect for the supreme spiritual masters, then good qualities will not develop and those that have developed will degenerate.

In this life, illness, evil spirits, untimely death and the like will come, and in future lives one will wander endlessly in the unfortunate realms.

Even if after hundreds (of rebirths) one obtains birth as a happy being, because of what must result in accordance with the cause, disrespect, one will be born in a leisureless state where not even the words "supreme Dharma" or "virtuous spiritual guide" are heard.

In brief, (a person) with breach of devotion to (his) spiritual guide will permanently wander in cyclic existence, especially in the unfortunate realms, and experience only suffering. Thus, he will have no chance to attain a high rebirth or liberation.

Since advantages and disadvantages such as these are beyond comprehension, and since it is evident that the roots of the accumulation of merit lie here as well, isn't it time to stop finding fault (with my Gurus) and devote (myself to them) with reverence and faith?

Practicing Faith, the Root (of Virtue)

It was stated in the Sutras that all spiritual guides who show us the path are like (reflections of) the single moon in the sky that effortlessly and simultaneously appear in all the earth's waters.

Similarly, the wisdom of all the Buddhas effortlessly and simultaneously appears as the body of form, the body of utility, ordinary spiritual guides, and so forth, in whatever forms are (suited) to tame all pure and impure disciples.[23]

It is said particularly in many of the Tantras that in the eon's decline, the all-pervading lord, holder of the vajra, having shown himself in the form of ordinary virtuous spiritual guides, will lead all degenerate beings.

For that reason, whatever forms and actions they may manifest, there is no doubt that in actuality all the victorious ones of the ten directions, in order to lead us to the path of liberation, are revealing (themselves) in the forms that tame us.

Although these (forms and actions) appear to have faults, (our perception is) similar to that of Devadatta, Leg-gar, and the philosophers who challenged (Buddha Shakyamuni). They (incorrectly) perceived that master teacher, who had eliminated all faults and consummated all good qualities, as being a mass of defects.[24]

Just as a man with jaundice perceives a (white) conch as yellow, so do I, veiled with obstructions and bad deeds, always perceive that which is faultless as having faults. In reality, however, how can (Buddha) possess faults?

What certainty is there that those (forms and actions) which appear to have faults were not shown for a purpose? As is stated (in the Sutras and Tantras), for the sake of sentient beings the victorious ones have shown themselves as emanations of demons and so forth. While I am not free from bad deeds and obstructions, even if all the Buddhas were actually to come before me, I would not have the good fortune to see their most excellent bodies adorned with the major and minor marks. I only (would see them in the form of ordinary spiritual masters such as) those who appear to me now.

Thus, all the actions of my spiritual protectors which appear to have faults are either the illusory appearance of my own bad deeds or they have been shown for a purpose.

For that reason, however they may appear to me, (these spiritual protectors) have actually eliminated all defects and consummated all good qualities. Each is the essence of all the victorious ones of the innumerable pure realms combined.

Remembering the Kindness (of my Spiritual Protectors)

Not only are my spiritual protectors the very essence of all the victorious ones, but their kindness (to me) is much greater than that of all the Buddhas because they always nurture me with the nectar of supreme Dharma.

For example, if someone provided bail for a man suffering in prison and gave him a place to stay with the most prized luxuries, that would indeed be an act of great kindness.

The spiritual masters extend great kindness by showing me how to remain free from the three unfortunate realms, that I may temporarily enjoy the glorious endowments of gods and men as I desire.

Furthermore, by skilfully showing the unsurpassable methods to overcome all encumbrances of cyclic existence and solitary transcendence, they lead me to the supreme state of the three bodies. Why wouldn't this kindness be greater (than that shown to the prisoner)?

The Buddha said that the kindness of someone who has taught a single verse (of Dharma) cannot be repaid even by making offerings for as many eons as the number of words in that verse. Who then can measure the kindness of (a spiritual master) who has shown the complete noble path?

(Because of) the kindness of the venerable spiritual masters (I renounced) secular life which is like a fiery pit and entered into the religious life. Dwelling in seclusion with righteous and straightforward conduct, I experienced an unequalled taste, the nectar of supreme Dharma.[25]

Because of the kindness of the supreme spiritual protectors, I received and gained confidence in the teachings of the Gentle Guru Protector (Je Tsong Khapa), which are difficult to find even when sought for many thousands of eons.

For these reasons my spiritual guides are:

—protectors who save me from the unfortunate realms
—helmsmen who take me across the ocean of cyclic existence
—guides who lead me to the upper realms and liberation
—physicians who cure the chronic disease of mental afflictions
—rivers that extinguish the great fire of suffering
—lamps that dispel the darkness of ignorance
—the sun that reveals the path to liberation
—liberators who free me from the prison of cyclic existence
—clouds that shower the rain of supreme Dharma
—relatives who help me and protect me from harm
—parents who always care for me with love.

The Way to Please (the Gurus) through one's Conduct

All the happiness and well-being of worldly people and those who have transcended the world are (due to) the kindness of the spiritual masters. Although this kindness can never be fully repaid, in order to return (some of) it, I shall try to please them.

Just as farmers exert themselves to plant seeds in a fertile field, why don't I exert myself in offering homage and wealth to the Gurus, the supreme field? Even though they do not look for offerings and esteem, I should do this in order quickly to complete my collection of merit.

(The Buddha) said that there is far greater merit in making offerings to a single hair on the body of a spiritual master who teaches one the unerring path than to honor and make offerings to the entire assemblage of exalted ones, hearkeners, solitary victors, Bodhisattvas, and each and every Buddha.

Many sages such as Naropa, Mila-repa, Drom-tonpa, Sakya Panchen, and Ja-yulwa developed their good qualities by giving up without reluctance their bodies, lives and wealth for their gurus.

Therefore, I shall strive reverently to serve (my gurus) with body and speech by praising and speaking respectfully to them, massaging and bathing them, rising and prostrating to them, and offering whatever cherished wealth I have.

The supreme (conduct) of the three doors that most pleases the gurus is to make great undiverted effort, day and night, on the stages of the complete, unerring path. I shall, therefore, please them with the offering of practice in accordance with their instructions.

(O Spiritual Masters), please bestow inspiring strength so that I may be able to do this.

Understanding (the Meaning of) Leisure and Endowments

From beginningless (time) until now, in my previous (lives) I wandered throughout the three realms of cyclic existence, taking (birth in) countless bodies of animals, hungry ghosts and hell beings.

(My) suffering was interrupted only rarely when I took birth as a happy being, and even then I was usually born in dark eons, without the teachings of Buddha. There were times when I wandered through irreligious lands; in some lives I was (born) retarded or dumb.

On some (occasions) I was a person with deluded views; on others I was misled by false teachers. There were times which I passed with a semblance of Dharma, and others in which I was a dull, ignorant person.

Because of the great kindness of the spiritual masters, now I am free from fears of the three unfortunate realms, have obtained the most excellent birth of a human being in this world, and have met with an auspicious eon—a time of light.

I have been born with intelligence and complete sense faculties in a land where the glorious supreme Dharma flourishes. I have gained conviction in the three baskets of Dharma and met a spiritual master who is just like Lord Buddha.

I have obtained oral instructions on the complete unerring path, clear inner wisdom which distinguishes what is to be adopted and renounced, a mind well directed to the supreme Dharma, and all favorable conditions such as food, clothing and wealth.

Thus, by the force of an ocean of merit that I previously accumulated, I have now obtained the birth of a human being possessing this excellent foundation—all eighteen factors of leisure and endowments.

Contemplating the Great Value of Leisure and Endowments

The value of a billion worlds filled with precious jewels is enormous and yet insignificant in comparison to (the value of) this body which is the complete foundation of leisure and endowments. With this good foundation I can easily acquire, for a time, whatever I desire of all the auspiciousness of gods and men in the upper realms, as I have wished.

With this foundation I can easily obtain, if I wish, not merely higher levels of cyclic existence but also a life with the eight matured advantages for practising to attain the glorious states of definite goodness.

With this (foundation) I can transcend the impure world and its inhabitants and go to whatever completely pure realm I wish such as the spacious and blissful realm of Tushita.[26]

Moreover, with this good foundation, if I wish I can permanently dispel all the sufferings of cyclic existence—birth, aging, sickness, death, etc.—and attain the bliss of liberation. With this good foundation, if I practise I can completely eliminate the two obstructions together with their latencies and effect the effortless consummation of all good qualities—the state of the three bodies.

With this foundation which possesses the six special elements, if I rely upon the highest Tantric practice I can attain during this short life the two supreme bodies—the actual state of unification.

For these reasons, whether one considers the temporary or ultimate meaning of this good foundation of leisure and endowments, because of its extremely great benefits, the venerable gurus have said that it is superior to a wish-fulfilling gem.

Considering that I have now obtained a foundation such as this, it is madness to be attracted to fruitless work for this life rather than follow the path to higher realms and liberation.

Now that I can practise whatever I wish (and even attain) the dual goal, failing to begin my practise immediately is similar to not taking a wish-fulfilling gem after reaching the Island of Jewels.

Extending (my motivation beyond) actions for this life and training my mind day and night in the stages of the bodhi path, the ultimate Dharma, I shall make meaningful this foundation of leisure and endowments which I have obtained.

Contemplating the Difficulty of Finding Leisure and Endowments

Dru-gu, who was lame, once rode a wild ass.[27] Similarly, I have obtained this foundation (of leisure and endowments) and will never have this opportunity again.

In general, to attain a happy rebirth, I must accumulate the respective virtuous causes, but since it is difficult for my mind to develop virtuous thoughts, it is likewise extremely difficult to attain a happy rebirth.

In particular, to obtain leisure and endowments, I must acquire the individual causes (for each of) their eighteen factors. Since the acquisition of such causes is extremely rare, how could complete leisure and endowments, the result, not be rare?

Even if (once) in a hundred (lives) I acquire every cause for obtaining leisure and endowments, there are still many conditions in my mental continuum which destroy these (causes) such as anger, deluded views and abandoning Dharma.

Even if (these causes) are not destroyed by such conditions, since the force of my deluded mind and erroneous conduct is strong and the force of my virtuous mind and good conduct—the path—is weak, which results are certain to ripen first?

Like a star at noon, the teachings of the Victorious Lord occur only rarely in this world. By considering this, (I can see how) extremely rare it is to obtain an excellent foundation of leisure and endowments.

"The beings (who sink) down to unfortunate realms (are as numerous as) the particles of dust on this vast earth, whereas the beings (who rise) up to happy (realms are few), like the particles of dust on my fingernail." Was this not said by our protector, the master teacher, who always spoke the truth without deception?

(The Buddha) said that if one compares the infinite number of hell beings, hungry ghosts, and animals (to the number of) beings with a happy birth, it seems there are only a few in the form of gods and men.

How many ignorant creatures are there in an area of ground the size of a tarpaulin? In a city, the number of people, however many, even if great, is (seldom more than) a hundred thousand.

Among people, consider which are more numerous and which are less; those who have entered the door of Dharma or those who have not entered that (door). Again, among those who wish to practise Dharma, consider which are more numerous: those who have complete leisure and endowments (or those who do not).

The Victorious One compared the (rarity of complete leisure and endowments) to a turtle sticking his neck through the opening of a wooden yoke floating on the vast ocean, a bean sticking to the wall of a crystal palace, a star seen in the blue sky at noon, a mustard seed remaining on the tip of a needle, and so forth. With many such examples to make the meaning clear, he taught that the body with a foundation of leisure and endowments is (extremely) rare.

As shown by such examples and those of cause and result, this good foundation of leisure and endowments is extremely difficult to find, yet I have found it this once. Dare I go on without taking advantage of its essential meaning?

At this time, free from the eight leisureless states, I have obtained a life with leisure and endowments, but because I have been distracted by appearances and have not taken advantage of the essence, my return to the unfortunate realms has begun.

This is like returning to my homeland from the Island of Jewels, empty-handed. What could be more stupid? What could be a greater loss?

In general, to obtain a life with leisure and endowments is rare. In particular, to meet with the teachings of the gentle (Guru) protector is rare, to have as a refuge a fully qualified spiritual master is rare, and to have the Dharma, both complete and unerring, is rare.

To have discriminating wisdom within is rare, a mind which can properly utilize the supreme Dharma is rare, a friend who strives for liberation is rare, and sustenance obtained in accordance with Dharma is rare.

At this time when so many rarities have been brought together, if I do not renounce all thoughts and actions for this life (alone) and follow the path to upper realms and definite goodness, there can be no greater loss.

Now, in order to benefit the mother beings who have time and again cared for me with kindness, I shall complete the practices of the profound path without being overcome by wavering (motivation).

O Spiritual Masters, please bestow inspiring strength (so that I may accomplish) this goal.

Contemplating the Certainty of Death

A good life that is truly meaningful is always difficult to find and even when found is impermanent and will quickly be destroyed like a dewdrop which clings to the tip of a blade of grass.

In this limitless cyclic existence of three realms, whether I take a body in a happy or unfortunate rebirth, in the end that (body) will not go beyond death.

In whatever place I dwell, whether in the upper regions of space, on the ground, in the ocean, or in the crevices of great mountains, I will not be free from my enemy, the Lord of Death.[28]

In previous times when eons have come to an end, in this time when the five degenerations are becoming widespread, and again in future times whenever (I live), there is no chance to avoid being trampled by the Lord of Death.

The gods Brahma, Shiva and Vishnu, the powerful strength of a world ruler's armies, the force of a sage's truth, the miracles, mantras and devices of magicians, and whatever other means (there may be) cannot turn death away.

Even if I pay as ransom an expanse filled with the wealth and possessions of a billion worlds, I will not be released. Even if the venerable Medicine Buddha treats me, there will be no remedy for this enemy, the Lord of Death.

If I carefully examine all the beings, distinguished and lowly, who lived in the past, (I find that) now only their names remain. And of all the beings who are living now, every one of them will someday pass away.

My life is not becoming longer; it is running out without pausing for a moment. Like the flame of a burning lamp, how can it continue and never be extinguished?

From the very first (moment) of my life in the womb, I go to my death without stopping, like a cascading waterfall. Is it not an illusion to think that I will continue to live (without ever dying)?

If someone, while being rushed to the place of his execution, is served desirable objects of the five senses, would there be a reason for him to be pleased?

Similarly, without pausing for a moment, I am rushing into the presence of death; so even if numerous things that I really desire are gathered (before me), would this situation delight me?

Since my present status, house, relatives, friends, possessions, and even this body must all pass away without remaining for long, to what am I attached in this dream-like present?

The years, months, nights, and all time are as fleeting as the shadows of the sun; since they are transient, how can death not come soon?

From birth to now so many years have passed and for the remainder of this life I shall be distracted by sleep and so forth. Since the time left to practise Dharma is so short, is it really enough?

In the same way, if I examine even a single day and night to see if I properly contemplate the Dharma or distract myself more, it is clear that because (I waste) my time, I do not have enough.

Since under no condition (can death) be turned away, in the end I shall surely die. Moreover, because I may die soon without having had enough time, why am I not definitely striving to (practise) the Dharma now?

Contemplating the Uncertainty of the Time of Death

It is definite that I shall eventually die, and furthermore, there is no certainty that on this very day I shall not lose my life, be laid in the grave, and find my mind in the intermediate state.

In previous (ages, people of this world) have had immeasurable lifespans; later they could live to no more than ten years. At present there is no order in which old and young (die). What certainty is there now to the life (span of the people) in this world?[29]

(Sometimes) in the morning a person is alive, then later in the day he is not. When going to sleep he is alive, but when it is time to awake he is not. Just now a person is alive, and now again he is not. The impermanent condition of life is fearful indeed.

Every day head-on collisions occur and (people) fall into ravines. Boats capsize in water and (people) are burned by fire. Houses cave in and (people) are thrown by horses. Bodies, legs, and arms are broken and (people) are injured by weapons.

Harm from human and non-human enemies, the four hundred and twenty-four different sicknesses, the eighty thousand types of evil spirits and obstacles, and so forth—the external and internal conditions of death are many.

As the five degenerations are now increasing, the means for sustaining life are becoming difficult to acquire, and since medicine is often ineffective, the conditions supporting life are few.

Indigestible food becomes poison and unsuitable medicine brings sickness. Since even the conditions supporting life may become those of death, what confidence can I have in the conditions that sustain my life in this (world)?

The various conditions for death (such as) the illnesses of air affect my life, just as (wind moves the flame of) a lamp; (yet still) I think and act as if I will remain forever. I am definitely under the evil influence of grasping for permanence.

The bodies and lives of people are (as tenuous) as bubbles in water; since even minor circumstances destroy them, looking forward to a long life is a great error.

All enduring things such as the earth, Mount Meru, the four continents, and the oceans will eventually come to destruction. What certainty is there that this body, (as fragile) as a clay pot, will not fall apart at this very moment?

Now I am healthy and happy, but because my enemy, the Lord of Death, will come as unexpectedly as a cloud in the sky, this is not the time to remain at ease.

Since it is uncertain which of these two will come first—the dawn of tomorrow or my body and mind of the intermediate state and the next life—is it not worthwhile to energetically practise the supreme Dharma now?

The Way to Contemplate that when one Dies, Nothing but Dharma can Help

When I am seized by my enemy, the Lord of Death, then even if all sentient beings in the three realms gather round me as friends and relatives, I shall be powerless to take a single one of them with me.

Even if I own a billion worlds filled with heaps of the seven precious materials, I have no way to bring into my next life so much as a sesame seed from that wealth.

Even the body with which I was born is left behind on a mattress and bedding while, by the force of the wind from my virtuous and evil deeds, my mind is carried to a place in one of the six realms.

For this reason, at the time of death, my body, possessions, relatives and friends cannot help me at all. The only thing which is really beneficial is the infallible savior, supreme Dharma.

I shall therefore turn away from the meaningless, dream-like activities of this life, and through the stages of the bodhi path, the essence of Dharma, I shall practise to attain the glorious state of bodhi.

(O Spiritual Masters), please bestow inspiring strength so that I may be able to do so.

The Way to Meditate upon the Sufferings of the Hot Hells

Alas, the meaningful life, so difficult to find, is impermanent and will soon be destroyed. And after death I have no freedom to choose where I shall be reborn, because that is determined by (my previous) deeds.

The force of my non-virtuous deeds is very strong, and the force of my virtuous deeds very weak. If I fall into the fearful abyss of the unfortunate realms, how shall I bear the suffering?

Many miles below the earth live the hell beings. The bottom (of hell) is a blazing ground of burning hot iron. The sides are walls of scorching iron. The sky above is covered with flames. Each individual hell is also made of burning hot iron and surrounded by a wall secured by four doors.

In the Reviving Hell, the sentient beings become furious with each other. With various weapons that arise from their deeds, they strike each other and collapse unconscious. Then from the sky a voice commands, "All of you, revive!" Immediately they revive and after rising they repeatedly experience the same suffering as before.

In the Black Line Hell, (the beings) are seized by many of Yama's fearsome men and are forced to lie on the ground of burning hot iron. Their limbs are stretched out like a tarpaulin and their cherished bodies are branded with many criss-crossed black lines. Then they experience the suffering of being cut and split open by various weapons along those (black lines).

In the Hell of Mass Destruction, (the beings) are herded between two massive iron mountains resembling the heads of lions, tigers, and so forth. Then the two mountains smash together, crushing them, and a river of blood gushes forth. They are forced into large iron machines which mash them to a pulp like sugar cane. They are crushed by huge mountain-like boulders which fall from the sky, smashing their flesh and blood into paste.

In the Wailing Hell,[30] the sentient beings flee in search of a place (of safety). They are admitted into one and two-level houses of iron that explode into flames. As soon as this happens, the doors slam shut and there is no way for them to escape. Enveloped by flames, their bodies burn and smoke and they pass the days and nights screaming.

In the Hot Hell, (the beings) are fried like fish on a broad expanse of flaming bronze. Flames leap out from all the apertures of their bodies as they are skewered from the anus through to the top of the head with fiery spikes. They are forced to lie down on blazing iron ground where they are pounded with iron sledge hammers.

In the Extremely Hot Hell, (the beings) are pierced through with flaming tridents and their bodies are clothed in sheets of red-hot iron. They are boiled in a huge bronze cauldron of molten copper and when flesh and bones separate, their skeletons are spread out on the ground, the flesh and skin grow back, and again they are cooked as before.

In the Hell of Unceasing Torment, tremendous exploding fireballs hurtle down from the four directions and burn (the beings') flesh, skin, tendons and bones to the marrow like the wick of a burning lamp. Only by the cries emitted through the force of their suffering can one know that these are actually sentient beings.

(The hell beings) have searing iron ashes pressed into their hands and are forced to dance in flaming embers. They descend from high mountains of blazing iron and are forced to ascend them again. Their tongues are pulled from their mouths, stretched out, and staked down with iron spikes. They are thrown down by Yama's men who open their mouths with glowing hot forceps, stuff flaming iron balls into their mouths and pour boiling molten bronze down their throats.

The Way to Meditate upon the Sufferings of the Neighboring Hells

Outside the doors of each of the eight hot hell realms are the neighboring hells with many terrors. In the pit of fiery ash, when (the beings) put down their feet, they sink to their knees and the skin and flesh are destroyed. When they pick up (their legs, the skin and flesh) immediately grow back and again they must experience the same (suffering).

In the swamp of excrement (as foul) as a corpse, (the beings) fall in and sink down to their necks. Bugs with sharp mandibles that live in the mire burrow and eat to the marrow. On the road covered with upturned, razor-sharp sword blades, the beings step down and their feet are cut into pieces. When they lift up (their legs, the feet) grow back. This they do again and again.

In the forest of sword leaf (trees, when the beings) arrive they seek shade and sit down. Then many sharp sword leaves fall from the trees and cut off their limbs and other appendages. After being wounded they collapse stricken to the ground where dogs tear and eat the flesh from their bodies.

In the Grove and Thorny Trees, the beings are forced to climb up and down iron tree trunks bristling with iron thorns. When they climb up, the thorns face downwards and when they climb down, the thorns bristle upwards, piercing their limbs and other appendages. Many iron-beaked crows land on their heads and peck out their eyes.

The scalding hot river of glowing molten lava has a strong current and no ford. When beings fall into that furiously boiling (torrent), all their skin, flesh and blood are destroyed. Along the banks there are men brandishing staffs with iron hooks. With their staffs they push back anyone who tries to come out, (and) with the iron hooks they fling (anyone who is out) back in. After knocking them over, they ask (the beings), "What do you want?" Those who say they are hungry or thirsty are given (red hot iron) balls or molten copper.

Thus, the suffering of beings in the great hells is completely unbearable and lasts not just for a short time but for countless eons. As long as (the force of) their non-virtue goes unspent, for just that long must (these hell beings) continue to live. Since this was taught (by Buddha, yet still) I am not terrified, what is my mind, inert matter?

The Way to Meditate upon the Sufferings of the Cold Hells

Four hundred thousand miles from the realm of the hot hells there are eight cold hells. (These hells) have ground covered with ice on which snow whirls in a blizzard. They are hemmed in on all sides by snow mountains and enveloped in pitch-darkness. Freezing winds blow upwards.

(The beings) in this place wear no clothes. Their naked bodies shiver, hunch over, and completely shrivel up. The wind causes hundreds of thousands of blisters to erupt and when they burst, pus runs out. (The beings) make the miserable sound "ah choo" and their teeth chatter. From contact with the terrible cold their bodies turn blue, then red, and crack into pieces.

These sensations of extreme cold are not (experienced) for just a few days. If one threw out a seed every hundred years from a large bin holding a ton of sesame, (the time it would take for) that to run out equals the lifespan for a being in the Blistering Hell. In the other seven (cold hells, the beings live) twenty times (longer than in the preceding one). Since (the Buddha) taught (the existence of all this), what assurance is there that I shall not be born in such a place? If I am born there, shall I be able to bear that suffering?

The Way to Meditate upon the Sufferings of Hungry Ghosts

Twenty thousand miles below this world is (the realm of) hungry ghosts, who become (as they are) because of miserliness. It has ground which is copper red in color as if scorched by the sun. It is a vast, depressing plain of misery, devoid of anything desirable. The beings there have bodies with parched throats, huge bellies, and skinny limbs; they resemble charred tree stumps.

(The hungry ghosts) with outer obstructions see fruit trees, water and so forth, but when they run to get them, it is like running after the water of a mirage. Wherever (they search, the food and water) disappear or appear to be filled with pus, blood, feces, urine, other disagreeable matter, or glowing embers. Or guards brandishing various weapons protect (the food and drink), not allowing them to have it.

The (hungry ghosts) with inner obstructions have bodies with stomachs as large as a mountain but mouths as small as the eye of a needle. Flames erupt (from the apertures of their bodies; their throats) are blocked by goiters. Even if they find food and drink, it does not fit in their mouths, and even if it fits, the flames in their mouths burn it up. (If it gets past their mouths, it is) blocked by their goiters and won't pass down their throats, and even if it gets loose, it doesn't fill their stomachs.

The (hungry ghosts) with obstructions in the food and drink itself are the "(ghosts) with garlands of flames"; whatever they eat or drink bursts into flames and burns them. (The ghosts) who eat filth lack any opportunity to enjoy good food and drink; instead they partake only of foul-smelling, unclean things such as feces, urine, spit, snot, vomit, pus, blood, and so forth.

Furthermore, with their enormous bodies and tiny limbs, they become completely exhausted running after food. In the summer even moonlight feels hot to them, and in the winter even sunlight feels cold. If they so much as look at the ocean it dries up, and some have throats obstructed by knots. As their bodies and minds become increasingly tormented by pangs of hunger, they tear off their own flesh and eat it.

Not even hearing about food or drink, they are continually oppressed by the severe sufferings of extreme hunger and thirst, and this lasts not for just a short time. A month for humans is one day and night for them and they do not die for five hundred, five thousand, and some not even ten thousand of their own years. (All this the Buddha) taught. What shall I do if I am born in that place?

The Way to Meditate upon the Sufferings of Animals

The main abode of stupid animals is in the great ocean from the water's surface down to the floor. (Those beings have) no fixed (type of) body but vary in shape, color, size, and so forth. They are countless in number like a mound of barley heaped on the ground and they are so crowded together that even movement is difficult. They dwell in cavities of dark gloom.

Of those animals who live scattered throughout the regions of gods and men, some are tormented by hunger and thirst, some suffer from (extremes of) sun and wind which are difficult to endure, some live and die in darkness, some live in the dirt and on rocks, and others wallow in mires of excrement. Sometimes large ones swallow small ones and sometimes many small ones eat a large one.

They are killed in different ways for their meat and hides. They are loaded with heavy burdens for which they haven't the strength, and after being mounted, they are exploited and beaten. Their hair and even their organs are cut off. They are used for plowing, milking, and so forth. They are oppressed incessantly day and night with many unbearable sufferings.

It is not always certain that their lives will be short, for those with long lifespans can live for as much as an eon. (Arising) by the force of their (previous) deeds, their many different sufferings stupefy them. They are all very dull and ignorant, not knowing what should be adopted and what renounced. If I am born for an instant in such a woeful body, how shall I bear it?

The Practice of Going for Refuge

Going for refuge to anything other than the Three Jewels cannot protect me from the intolerable sufferings, so difficult to bear, of hell beings, hungry ghosts, and animals.

This is how the Three Jewels protect me: the Dharma is the actual savior which protects me from the fearful (sufferings of cyclic existence), the Buddhas are the master teachers of the Dharma, and the Sangha are my helpers in practising the Dharma.

For this reason, if from the depths of my heart I do not seek protection in the supreme infallible refuge, the Three Jewels, then I shall have no way to be free from the dangers of the fearful abyss of the lower realms and particularly of cyclic existence.

I shall earnestly take refuge from this moment on, because if I fall into the unfortunate realms, then even if I cry out hundreds of times, there will be no savior to protect me at that (time), in that (place).

Therefore, from now on, I and all other beings
Go for refuge to the supreme master teachers, the Buddhas,
Go for refuge to the supreme Dharma, which is taught by them,
Go for refuge to the Sangha, who practise the (Dharma).

Recite the verse of actually going for refuge, "Therefore, from now on,..." three, seven, or more times.

Having affirmed my refuge in the Three Jewels like this, I must properly follow the instructions of going for refuge.

Having taken refuge in the master teacher, I shall not take refuge in other than (exalted) teachers nor worldly gods.[31] I shall make offerings and abandon irreverence by venerating even an image of the master teacher as the Buddha.

Having gone for refuge to the Dharma, I shall not devote myself to what is not Dharma, I shall renounce harmful thoughts and actions towards living beings and show respect by never stepping over even a single letter of the supreme Dharma.

Having taken refuge in the Sangha, I shall not rely on non-Buddhist philosophers, friends with deluded views, and so forth.

I shall have neither attachment nor hatred. I shall respect those who merely wear the saffron robes as I do the actual exalted Sangha.

From understanding the various qualities of the Three Jewels and the difference between [Buddhist and non-Buddhist] (refuge), I shall go for refuge again and again to the Three Jewels. Remembering their kindness, I shall assiduously make offerings to them, offering the first portion of my food and drink as well.

With constant remembrance of compassion, I shall influence other beings to take refuge in the Three Jewels. Respectfully making offerings and requests to the Three Jewels at all times, I shall abandon means other than them.

Knowing the benefits of going for refuge, I shall do so three times during the day and three times at night. Keeping the Three Jewels on the crown of my head, I shall never abandon them, even as a joke or for the sake of my life.

By going for refuge, I enter the door of the Victorious One's doctrine and establish a basis for taking the three pure (types of) vows. My obstructions and (erroneous) deeds are diminished or exhausted and I acquire extensive merit. I cannot fall into the unfortunate realms or be harmed by non-humans.

Furthermore, whatever I wish can be accomplished and I can quickly (attain) Buddhahood. Since (Buddha) said that the benefits are inconceivable, I shall take heartfelt refuge and never disregard these instructions.

The Way to Develop Faith of Conviction about Deeds and their Results[32]

If I fear the sufferings of the unfortunate realms, I must carefully check the actions of my three doors and then, with firm memory, alertness and mindfulness, practise engaging in even the smallest white deeds and turning away from even the smallest black deeds.[33]

All my unbearable sufferings are solely the results of deeds which I, myself, have accumulated. Since others have not caused me to experience (my suffering), I shall strive to accomplish good and abandon evil now.

For example, from planting individual seeds of wheat, barley, beans, millet, rice, and so forth in a fertile field, individual sprouts arise without deviation (according to the type of seed planted).

Similarly, happiness and suffering, in general, arise from deeds, (and in particular), even the slightest happiness and suffering always arise without deviation from virtue and non-virtue, because it is impossible for anything to arise without a cause or from unsuitable causes.[34]

Small seeds grow into large crops. Similarly, in countless successive lives, limitless results of happiness and misery arise from even the tiniest individual virtuous and non-virtuous causes.

Just as crops do not grow when seeds are not planted, if virtuous and non-virtuous deeds are not accumulated, no results of happiness and misery whatsoever occur, because one cannot receive (results) from deeds one has not committed.

If seeds are planted and there is nothing to obstruct them, then crops will undoubtedly arise. Similarly, if virtue is collected and not overcome by destructive forces such as anger and so forth, then resulting happiness will occur without being lost.[35]

Likewise, if non-virtue is accumulated and not counteracted by the purifying forces—confession and so forth—[36] then resulting suffering will occur without being lost.

Thus, deeds individually (produce) definite and increasing (results); (if deeds are) not committed, (results) are not received; once they are committed, (their force) is never lost.

Like a person full of desire and unsatisfied with his wealth, I shall earnestly strive to accumulate only good deeds, diligently (collecting) even the smallest. I shall be careful not to destroy with anger and so forth the (good deeds) that I have already performed.[37]

I shall never commit any non-virtue, abandoning even the smallest. I shall be as afraid (of bad deeds) as I would be of a poisonous snake (coiled) in my lap. With the four forces I shall be sure to purify (the non-virtue) I have already collected.

In particular, I shall not be content with mere (attainment of) high rebirths, because that is greatly surpassed by the attainment of bodhi. I shall, therefore, diligently practise to acquire all the causes for attaining a most excellent life with the eight matured advantages.

(O Spiritual Masters), please bestow inspiring strength so that I may be able to do this.

Teachings in Common with a Person of Intermediate Scope[38]

The Way to Meditate on the Human Sufferings

If I abandon evil and strive for virtue, then I will surely attain a high rebirth. But if I do not attain the state of liberation, which is the complete cessation of all the suffering of cyclic existence, I can have no peace of mind, because again I will wander in the unfortunate realms. Furthermore, I will have no chance to be happy even (when I attain a high) rebirth, for essentially the nature (of cyclic existence) is suffering.

For humans, the womb is filled with germs and the stinking filth of pus, blood, and the like. It is horrible to be confined in such a dark, cramped, uncomfortable place. (As a fetus), my body is curled as if bound and completely wrapped up in the placenta. Because of my mother's behavior and so forth, I experience many sufferings for long periods.[39]

From the full maturation of my deeds I am born. (The force of) air turns me upside down; then from the cervix which is fetid, unclean, and very narrow like a machine made of bones, I am born in extreme misery, violently and with unbearable sensations of roughness. The misery of birth is an unwanted suffering that falls like rain; it is truly something to be feared.

My body, at first so youthful, gradually changes. (Then), as if (suddenly) transformed, it is hunched. My color is poor, my hair white, my gait unsteady even when I walk on level ground. As my muscle tone deteriorates, I am covered with wrinkles and my skin hangs loosely. As my rows of teeth crumble, I crave food. I speak indistinctly and become extremely forgetful.

I become blind and hard of hearing, and have trouble sitting down and getting up; others treat me with contempt. Even food and drink are difficult to enjoy or digest; everyone is disgusted (with me). Daily I am oppressed with the distressing thought that now my health is deteriorating and soon I shall die. The suffering of aging is truly depressing.

When I am stricken by illness with my elements in disorder,[40] moving around is difficult and I become bedridden. I constantly moan with severe pain and do not pass a day or night without crying. Unable to enjoy what I like, I am given disagreeable food, drink, medicine, and so forth. I must undergo operations, burns and other treatments as agonizing as the continual torment of sickness.

My complexion pales and my voice becomes feeble. Unable to rise, I cannot do what I want. Because I am in the grip of illness, my environment, body, possessions, attendants and friends all seem like enemies. I pass the day and night despondently, increasingly oppressed by the wretchedness of dreading death from my ailments. The suffering of sickness is truly vicious.

By physical illness or other conditions, I am heading into the mouth of the Lord of Death. When I am seized by the violent illness of death, I lie down for the last time on a bed. Doctors are no help; prayers do not turn (death) away; I and others give up hope for my life. Sobbing relatives and friends gather around and wash my face with tears.

I utter my final words and then my corpse is prepared for the grave. My nose stops functioning, my mouth goes dry, my eyes roll upward, and I gasp for breath. (When these things happen) one after another, what can I do? I am tormented with anguish from attachment to my relatives, body, possessions and friends, and filled with regret for my evil deeds. With the violent pain of my life functions disintegrating, my arms and legs flail, and so forth. The suffering of death is truly frightening.[41]

These four enemies—birth, aging, sickness and death—turn the wheel (of cyclic existence and) torment me. And since there are many other sufferings in between them as well, I have no chance to remain happy. Confronted with the horrors of dreading hostile enemies, robbers, carnivorous beasts, non-humans, fires, floods, and so forth, my mind is imprisoned in a dungeon of misery.

Heartbroken and with deepest regret, I am separated without any choice from my relatives, possessions, and circle (of friends). When this (happens) the memory of (them) brings anguish. Whatever I utter comes out in sobs and choked with tears I faint. I pound my fists, tear my hair, can barely speak, and refuse to eat.

(Many) farm but do not reap a harvest; (many raise livestock but (the herds) do not thrive. (Many) enter commerce but do not make a profit; (many) beg or borrow but their hopes are not fulfilled. (Most of us) search with numerous hardships for the things we desire but do not find them; instead, the things we do not want such as frost, drought, disputes, attachment, litigation, and so forth fall on us.

The poor must work in such places as factories. They are oppressed as the servants and slaves of others. The affluent are always troubled with trying to protect and increase their wealth. Moreover, those who are hot, cold, hungry, thirsty and impoverished fight and argue among one another. Even we in the human realm are disturbed by so much suffering that it is similar to being in the unfortunate realms.

The Way to Meditate upon the Sufferings of the Demigods

The demigods (desire) all the wealth and auspiciousness of the gods (and so they) are mentally tormented by flames of jealousy which pierce their hearts like a thorn. Thus, they fight with the gods and experience unbearable suffering based upon their desires. Although they possess wisdom, they lack the good fortune to follow the path to liberation because of their matured obstructions.[42]

The Way to Meditate upon the Sufferings of the Desire Realm Gods

The desire realm gods have superlative abodes, bodies and possessions (until) suddenly their radiant complexions fade, they become displeased with their lounges, their flower garlands wither, their garments stink, and their bodies perspire as never before. Then when the symptoms of impending death seize them, they are like human beings caught in the throes of death.[43]

They are torn from the things they most cherish—the palaces and surroundings made of jewels, food of nectar, friends and so forth.

Then, from knowing that they will pass on to another world and realizing where they will be reborn, they suffer long the unbearable misery of being separated from beauty.[44]

Moreover, they suffer when they fight the hosts of demigods: their extremities, limbs and torsos are cut to pieces and they are killed. Gods of lesser merit are intimidated when they see the grandeur of gods endowed with vast wealth; the powerful gods with (superior) strength rout the weak ones from their abode. In these and other ways they suffer.

In brief, with excessive attachment to their desires, (the desire realm gods) are like (beings who) continually drink salt water. Since they are always tormented with dissatisfaction, what opportunity do they have to be happy? Their elephant minds are completely crazed with the intoxicants—desire and craving. They have little chance to be subdued by the iron hook of peace, the supreme Dharma.

The Way to Meditate upon the Sufferings of the Gods in the Two Higher Realms[45]

The suffering (of gods) in the two higher realms is not directly experienced; it is latent. (These gods) possess mental afflictions and (other) obstructions, the root of their nearness to suffering. (Because) they lack control over the conditions of death, it is their nature always to be oppressed by the terrible suffering of conditional existence,[46] and thus, since again they must fall, they lack security.

In brief, whatever good life I obtain (whether that) of a god or man, it is similar to a bird soaring through the sky. When the force of my virtuous deeds is exhausted, again I suffer after falling to the realms of the hells, hungry ghosts or animals. Alas, even the grandeur of the upper realms is impermanent and deceptive by nature.

The Way to Contemplate the Six Sufferings[47]

(If) the flesh and bones of all bodies in which I have previously taken (birth) were preserved, they would equal (the size of) Mount Meru. If the blood and lymph were collected into one place, they would equal the breadth and depth of the ocean. I have been Brahma,

Kausikah and a world ruler. I have also taken (birth in) the ordinary bodies of gods and men. Although they are difficult to count, I have already relinquished them all, so what security is there in obtaining a body?

My worst enemy of previous lives becomes my friend in this life and tries to help me. My friend of previous (lives) becomes a real enemy in this life and tries to kill me. Even in this very life, from the early part to the latter part, in every year, month and day, moment by moment, friends change into enemies and enemies into friends, (each) bringing benefit and harm. How can they be trusted?

(In previous lives) I overpowered the forces of Brahma, Indra and a world ruler, but later I became a servant and a slave. I was the sun and the moon,[48] illuminating the four continents, but later I had to lie down in the dark cavity (of hell). I tasted the nectar of gods, but later I had to eat pus, blood and molten copper. I dwelled in (heavenly) jewelled palaces, but later I burned in the flaming iron houses (of hell).

I was served sensual offerings by the upper realm goddesses, but later I was harmed by the guards of hell. Early in my life I was proud of my wealth and power, but later in my life I was destitute, unable to find food. I was rich with costly silk garments and jewels, but when I died I went naked and empty-handed. Oh, of all the most excellent things obtainable in cyclic existence, are there any in which I should place my trust?

I have long known my Dharma companions, intimate friends and circle of relatives, and have grown fond of them. But eventually, like a hair pulled from butter, I will wander alone, to an unfamiliar place in the next world. Should I really place trust in companions and friends?

In previous lives, I (dwelled) in the palaces and gardens of the gods, enjoying the taste of ambrosia and youth. In the human realm, I have worn fine clothes, enjoyed (good) food and drink, been close to my friends and so forth. The number of times that I have enjoyed desirable objects of the five senses is more than equal to (the number of) dust particles (in this world). But while I've enjoyed (these things), my increasing desire has brought me much suffering. The suffering of dissatisfaction is indeed distressing.

(The Buddha) said that if the molten copper we drank as hell beings, the silt we (consumed) as worms, and filth we ate as dogs, pigs, and so forth were gathered, it would completely fill this world. Moreover, the tears we wept from the heaviness of our misery would be greater in extent than the ocean. This was taught (by Buddha), yet still I am not distressed, disgusted or afraid. What is mind made of, iron?

(The Buddha) taught that if this vast earth were turned into mud and then made into pellets about the size of juniper berries, even these could be fully counted, but there is no apparent beginning to (the births) a person has taken from his mother. Since this is beginningless, how can a limit be shown for (the number of times) that I have been born in cyclic existence? This I must carefully consider.

The Way to Contemplate the Three Sufferings[49]

Our bodies and minds are tormented not only by the suffering of misery. (The Buddha) taught that in the realms of cyclic existence, all contaminated[50] feelings which appear to be pleasant are (merely) the appearance of happiness and a (temporary) halt of suffering; their nature is not happiness. Especially (we in the realms of cyclic existence) are always bound by the suffering of conditional existence.

In brief, when I must carry a heavy load that is difficult to bear, there is no occasion for happiness. Similarly, as long as I must hold on to these contaminated aggregates,[51] I will have no chance to be happy. These (contaminated) aggregates are produced by the power of (my) previous deeds and mental afflictions, and they continuously possess the seeds of all my suffering and mental afflictions which will later develop.

These (contaminated aggregates) give rise to all my future rebirths and are the basis for all the suffering of this life— birth, aging, sickness, death, and so on. (The suffering of) misery and the suffering of change develop in the way that bubbles do from water.[52] (Contaminated aggregates) from their inception are determined by deeds and mental afflictions; their nature is unhappiness and suffering.

Therefore, if I do not attain the highest peace, cessation of all the suffering of my aggregates, then wherever I am born in the three realms among the six types of beings, it will be like living in a pit of thorns. Because the three sufferings are the nature (of cyclic existence), I will have no chance to be happy. Now is the time for me to gain freedom from this prison of cyclic existence.[53]

The Way to Contemplate the Process by which One is Caught up in Cyclic Existence and the Way to Practise the Path that Leads to Liberation.

Like a water wheel I have always circled round and round, helplessly (taking rebirths) among the six types of beings, and thus have been continuously afflicted with the three types of sufferings. I must consider the cause of all this.

From time without beginning, thoughts of "I, I" have been in the depths of my heart. Because of this terrible demon, grasping at self-existence,[54] I discriminate between myself and others and so I develop attachment and hatred. With attachment and hatred, I accumulate deeds and because of these deeds, I circle in cyclic existence.

Therefore, if I do not counteract my grasping at self-existence, I will not become free from cyclic existence, and since I must counteract it with the wisdom of realizing self-existencelessness, I shall practise the training of extraordinary wisdom.[55]

Furthermore, if my mind is distracted by dullness and agitation, I will not perceive (phenomena) according to (their) self-existentless true nature. Therefore, after pacifying (all) distractions, I must (practice) the training of single-pointed concentration on profound true nature.

It is impossible, moreover, to develop concentration while lacking memory, alertness and mindfulness. I must, therefore, practise (the training of) extraordinary morality, strictly disciplining my three doors with unwavering memory and alertness.

For this reason, (Buddha) said that the heavily laden crops of wisdom training (grow) from atop the sprouts of steadfast concentration, and that since the field in which they grow is morality itself, the (vows of) individual liberation are the root of Buddhist doctrine.

I shall therefore listen to instructions concerning the foundation of the (three) trainings—the (vows of) individual liberation. I shall develop respect for the master teacher and his precepts and with memory, alertness, and mindfulness, cultivate the antidote for each of my mental afflictions.

Tightly shutting the four doors through which moral downfalls occur, I will try never to transgress the precepts laid down by the peerless, compassionate master teacher. Thus, I will establish the root of (his) teachings (in my mind).

(O Spiritual Masters), please bestow inspiring strength so that I may be able to do this.

Teachings Concerning a Person of Great Scope

The Way to Contemplate Why One must Engage in the (Practices of the Great Vehicle)

If I practise the three trainings well, then I myself will definitely be liberated from the ocean of cyclic existence. But striving for my own liberation while ignoring the sentient beings oppressed in cyclic existence is like working to free only myself while ignoring my imprisoned mother. What could be more shameless than that? I must therefore liberate all sentient beings.

The Way to Practice Mental Equilibrium

At this time, however, all beings appear as friends, enemies or neutral, and clinging to those (appearances), I develop hatred for enemies, attachment for friends, and indifference for the beings who are neutral.

Those who now appear to be enemies have been my mother many times in former lives. They have nursed me with milk, cared for me with love, worked for my welfare, and protected me from all harm.

Those who now appear to be friends have been my worst enemy in former lives. Numerous times they beat, killed and ate me alive. (This is what Buddha) taught.

Those who now appear to be neutral have been my friends and enemies in many previous lives. With anger they troubled and harmed me and with compassion they considered my welfare countless times.

Therefore, among all those beings, to whom should I be attached? For whom should I feel hatred? Without discriminating with attachment and hatred, I shall now think of them all as my friends.

But if I think that because friends and enemies are so changeable it is incorrect to help or harm them and correct to remain indifferent, this is wrong.

All those who in former lives were my enemies harmed me in anger because they were deluded and did not know (that I have been their) parent; it was wrong (for them to harm me). In former lives as friends they helped me, and since this was right for them to do, why don't I help them in return?

The Way to Meditate upon Knowing (all Sentient Beings) as Mother

How is it that all sentient beings have actually been my mother? (They have been) because I have taken rebirths without beginning in an infinite number of bodies.

If I think, however, that since sentient beings are infinite, they could not all have been my mother, indeed they have been, for just as sentient beings are countless, so are my rebirths.

(My rebirths are countless) because no beginning (to them) can be shown. (It cannot be said) that my mind began at a certain (time or) in a certain (place). Consequently there is no apparent limit to the number of bodies in which I have taken birth.

Except for those occasions when I have taken supernormal birth or birth in warmth and moisture, all the bodies which I have taken were born from wombs or eggs.[56] Because in each of those births I must surely have had a father and mother, it logically follows that all (beings) have been my mother.

Moreover, it has been established by scriptural authority that all beings have been my mother, because the Omniscient One, who never lies, said, "I do not see any beings wandering throughout cyclic existence who have not previously been born in this place, who have not taken bodies like this, and who have not been each other's parents, siblings and relatives."

For these reasons, although I do not know all sentient beings in their transmigrations through birth and death, just as I do not recognize my parents of this life after they die, all of them have actually been my mother who nurtured me with kindness.

The Way to Meditate upon Remembering the Kindness (of Mother Sentient Beings)

When I think about how I've been cared for with kindness, (I should consider) how my mother of this life carried me in her womb for nine months and ten days as if she were holding a precious jewelled vessel.

In walking, lying, sitting, and all her activities she was extremely prudent and cautious about whatever might harm me. Not even partaking of the foods and drinks she preferred, she devoted herself to what was beneficial and assiduously gave up what was harmful (to me).

Then when she gave birth, without thinking about the intolerable suffering that she herself was experiencing, she cherished me as if she had found a wish-fulfilling gem. Thus, she was extremely kind in the beginning.

After I was born, my hair was tangled, I excreted filth unknowingly, and I could not recognize in the least what was beneficial or harmful. But with much effort (my mother) reared me.

She nursed me with her milk, held me close to the warmth of her body, and wrapped me in soft blankets. When walking she carried me on her back and when sitting she held me in her lap. With her tongue she fed me chewed up (food) and with her mouth she wiped off my snot.

With her hands she cleaned off my excrement. Murmuring, "Oh, my child," she rocked me in her arms. She cared for me with tender thoughts and looked upon me with loving eyes. She called me sweet names and greeted me with smiles.

She protected me from the dangers of fire, water and steep falls. She preferred to be sick herself than for me to be sick; she preferred to die herself than for me to die. With such heartfelt acts, she was extremely kind when (I was a baby).

As I gradually grew up, she taught me how to eat, drink, walk and sit. When I was cold she gave me clothes and when I was hungry she gave me food and drink. She suffered hardships and engaged in non-virtue (for my benefit).

Ungrudgingly she gave me money and other things, never allowing herself to use them. Thus, she was extremely kind throughout (my life). And not only in this life, but in many previous lives as well, she treated me with kindness in the same way.

Just as (my mother of) this life was kind to me, so all sentient beings of the (other) five realms were repeatedly kind to me when they were human.

Also, when I was born from the eggs and wombs of beings other than humans, they protected me from harm and helped me according to the level of their knowledge and ability. I cannot imagine (the extent of their kindness).

The Way to Meditate upon Repaying the Kindness (of Mother Sentient Beings)

All sentient beings have been so very kind to me that neglecting to repay (their) great kindness would be the most ignoble behavior. How can I not repay their kindness?

(Sentient beings) everywhere have minds that are crazed by the terrible demon, mental afflictions; they lack vision (to see) the path to liberation; they have lost their spiritual guides who have this vision; they totter with erroneous conduct at the abyss of the lower realms. How can I allow myself to neglect and abandon them?

All mother sentient beings have previously experienced the (contaminated) happiness of cyclic existence many times. But since it has deceived them, giving them this would not fully repay their kindness. I must therefore lead them to the bliss of liberation.

The Way to Meditate upon Love

All mother sentient beings desire happiness, but most of them do not know that the cause of happiness is virtue. (Of those who) know, (most) do not practise (virtue), and even (those who) try are unable to practise it because of their mental afflictions.

Since results are not encountered from deeds not performed, the beings in unfortunate realms are always devoid of happiness. And although the beings in happy realms perceive (their) suffering as happiness, even they lack true happiness.

How wonderful it would be if all sentient beings possessed the supreme bliss of the omniscient Buddhas and its cause, the noble paths. They must possess (these). (O Spiritual Masters), please bestow inspiring strength so that I may bring this about.

The Way to Meditate upon Compassion

All (mother sentient beings) do not want suffering but most of them do not know that the cause of suffering is non-virtue. (Of those who) know, (most) do not renounce (non-virtue), and even (those who) try are unable to renounce it.

(The force of) a deed is never lost and since (sentient beings) engage in non-virtue, as hell beings they are tortured by excessive heat and cold. As hungry ghosts they are oppressed continually by hunger and thirst. As animals they are tormented by extreme stupidity, exploitation and slaughter.

As humans they are disturbed by the sufferings of birth, aging, sickness and death. As demigods they are afflicted with jealousy, arguments and fights. As desire realm gods they are distressed by the terrible misery of death and transmigration. As form and formless realm (gods) they are (bound by) the suffering of conditional existence.

How wonderful it would be if (sentient beings) were separated now from all their suffering and its cause, mental afflictions. They must be separated (from these). (O Spiritual Masters), please bestow inspiring strength so that (I may bring) this about.

The Way to Meditate upon the Extraordinary Attitude

It is not sufficient merely to wish for all sentient beings to be separated from suffering and possess happiness. I myself must bring this about.

For this reason I must dispel the suffering of all sentient beings and bring them happiness, just as I must dispel the suffering of my mother of this life and bring her happiness.

All sentient beings want to be happy and never to suffer. They have all been my mother, all equally kind to me. Thus, they are all the same.

I shall therefore take the great responsibility of liberating every sentient being from all the encumbrances of cyclic existence and solitary peace and of leading them to the supreme state of omniscience.

The Way to Meditate upon the Development of Bodhi Mind

As I am under the power of deeds and mental afflictions and unsure of where I will be reborn, how can I assume the responsibility for liberating all sentient beings from cyclic existence and leading them to unsurpassable bodhi?

Not only do I lack this ability now, but even if I were to attain the state of an arhat as a hearkener or solitary victor, I would still be unable to lead all beings to the level of omniscience.

The two types of arhat in the Small Vehicle have eliminated only the obstructions of mental afflictions but not the obstructions to omniscience. Thus, they have rid themselves of only one class of faults and have acquired only one class of good qualities.

For that reason, they cannot accomplish the ultimate benefit for themselves, and although they do help some sentient beings, they are unable to work for the benefit of all.

In that case, who is able to liberate all sentient beings from the ocean of cyclic existence? Buddha alone has this ability—others do not.

No one other than Buddha has achieved the ultimate benefit for himself, which is complete cessation and knowledge, much less the (ultimate) benefit for others. Therefore, whichever of these two benefits I strive for, I must attain the supreme state (of Buddhahood).

If I attain that (supreme state, then I will possess) the qualities of (Buddha's) body. He is adorned with the marks of perfection, (his characteristics) are immutable, and he can simultaneously manifest many forms before each sentient being.

(I will possess) the qualities of (Buddha's) speech. He can answer with one syllable the simultaneous individual questions of all sentient beings (so that each understands) the meaning in his own language, and he expresses (the Dharma) from all the parts of his body.

(I will possess) the qualities of (Buddha's) mind. With (full) understanding he directly perceives the true nature of all phenomena, while (at the same time) he perceives each and every object of knowledge as clearly as something held in the palm of his hand.

(I will possess) the qualities of (Buddha's) compassion. It was stated (in the Sutras and Tantras) that a mother's loving care for her son does not equal even a hundredth part of (Buddha's) loving compassion for all sentient beings.

(I will possess. Buddha's) good activities. Without ever moving from the sphere of Dharma, he emanates whatever (form) will tame (each sentient being).[57] (Surpassing) a wish-granting tree and a wish-fulfilling gem, he effortlessly brings about whatever is desired.

Moreover, it is not that (Buddha) sometimes (brings about what is desired) and sometimes does not, but rather, for as long as sentient beings remain (in cyclic existence) he will continually bring about (whatever they need in accordance with their level of development).

Oh, if I attain that supreme state (of Buddhahood), then possessing such qualities, I will be able to work most effectively for each and every mother sentient being.

Thus, I will do whatever (is necessary) to attain ever so quickly this supreme state, the ultimate benefit for both myself and others. I must achieve this (supreme state). (O Spiritual Masters), please bestow inspiring strength so that I may (be able to) do this.

Then, (after developing bodhi mind), engage in the six perfections which are later (explained in this text).[58]

In order to meditate upon (the development of) bodhi mind by means of equalizing and exchanging self and others, first meditate upon equilibrium, perceiving (all sentient beings) as mother and remembering their kindness just as (explained) before. Then (meditate) as follows:

The Method of Equalising and Exchanging Self and Others

Since all sentient beings have been my kind parents, it would not be right for me to neglect them and cherish myself.

I can see that self-cherishing has been the cause of all my suffering and that cherishing others has been the cause of all my happiness.

Moreover, (Buddha) said that whatever happiness there is in cyclic existence and transcendence comes from wanting happiness for others, and whatever encumbrances there are in cyclic existence and solitary peace come from wanting happiness for oneself.

In brief, children are disturbed by waves of suffering because they cherish themselves. Haven't the Buddhas attained the state of perfect bliss because they cherish others?

So, if I wish never to suffer, I must give up self-cherishing. If I wish to enjoy unending happiness, I must strive to cherish others. May all the sufferings of my mothers together with the causes of their suffering ripen on me, and thus may they be free from all suffering and its causes.

May all of the temporary and ultimate happiness together with any virtue I have ripen on these beings, and thus may they all possess supreme bliss.[59]

Meditate in this way—loving (sentient beings) by sending (them your happiness) and having compassion by taking on (their suffering). Then practise the extraordinary attitude and the development of bodhi mind as (explained) previously and the six perfections as (explained) below.

The Way to Train in the Six Perfections

Attainment of the supreme state of Buddhahood will not be accomplished merely by thinking "may I attain it." I shall therefore take the Bodhisattva vows, endeavor to follow the practises, and engage in the activities of the spiritual sons.

— to teach the Dharma in whatever way is suitable without looking for offerings, respect, and so forth is the giving of Dharma.

— to protect beings from harm that comes from humans, non-humans, and the elements is the giving of fearlessness.

— to give whatever is needed without hoping for matured results in return is the giving of material things.

— from now on I will earnestly practise these three types of giving. (O Spiritual Masters), please bestow inspiring strength so that I may be able to do this.

— to refrain from transgressing any rules of the three types of vows I have taken is the morality of keeping vows.

— to develop in my mental continuum virtues such as the six perfections and to increase those that I have already developed is the morality of collecting virtue.

— to work for the welfare of others as befits them through the eleven ways to benefit sentient beings is the morality of helping sentient beings.

— from now on I will earnestly practise these three types of morality. (Oh Spiritual Masters), please bestow inspiring strength so that I may be able to do this.

Though all sentient beings rise up as enemies and revile me, (I must) examine (the situation) with a discerning mind and not become angry. In response to their harm, (I should) try to help them. This is the patience of composure in the face of all harm.

If for the sake of Dharma I must go without food, clothing, house and bed, contract illnesses and (experience) other undesirable things, (I should) gladly bear these sufferings. This is the patience of accepting suffering (in order to practise Dharma).

To develop heartfelt admiration and trust for praiseworthy objects such as the Three Jewels is the patience of a steadfast attitude towards (worthy) objects.

From now on I will earnestly practise these three types of patience. (O Spiritual Masters), please bestow inspiring strength so that I may be able to do this.

If I must remain many eons in the unfortunate realms for the sake of each sentient being, and remain a long time in cyclic existence to obtain all of Buddha's good qualities, I (should) do so joyfully without becoming depressed. This is armorlike effort.

Diligence in collecting in my mental continuum virtues such as the six perfections is the effort of collecting virtue.

Diligence in the eleven ways to benefit sentient beings is the effort of working for the welfare of sentient beings.

From now on I will earnestly practise these three types of effort. (O Spiritual Masters), please bestow inspiring strength so that I may be able to do this.

According to nature there are (two kinds) of deep concentration—mundane and transcendental.[60]

According to type there are three—perfect serenity, extraordinary insight, and the combination of both.

According to function there is (deep concentration which brings) bliss of body and mind, deep concentration which supports good qualities, and deep concentration which benefits sentient beings. From now on I will earnestly practise these three classes of deep concentration.

(O Spiritual Masters), please bestow inspiring strength so that I may be able to do this.

Comprehending true nature is (the wisdom of) realizing absolute truth.

Comprehending the five subjects is (the wisdom of) realizing relative truth.

Knowing how to accomplish unerringly the dual goal of all beings is wisdom.

From now on I will earnestly practise these three types of wisdom. (O Spiritual Masters), please bestow inspiring strength so that I may be able to do this.

Instructions of the Four (Ways) of Gathering Disciples

(These) are the skilful means for leading disciples: giving them material things, teaching them the Dharma with pleasing instruction, encouraging them to act according to the sense of those teachings, and in the same way that one has encouraged them to behave, (acting) in accordance with the teachings oneself.

From now on I will properly practise the four ways of gathering (disciples). (O Spiritual Masters), please bestow inspiring strength so that I may be able to do this.

The Way to Meditate upon Perfect Serenity

If I become adept at the Bodhisattva practices but do not realize true nature, then no matter how much I try, I will not be liberated from cyclic existence. I shall therefore strive to realize the correct view.[61]

Furthermore, if my mind is distracted by dullness and agitation, I cannot possibly perceive the profound meaning of true nature. I will therefore strive to accomplish single-pointed concentration on some mental object in order to eliminate dullness and agitation.[62]

There are five impediments to accomplishing (perfect serene) concentration: laziness which is a lack of enthusiasm for meditating with concentration, forgetting the object of meditation, dullness and agitation, not applying (the antidotes to them), and applying (the antidotes unnecessarily).

The antidotes for laziness are: faith which perceives the advantages of perfect serene concentration, the aspiration brought on by that (faith) to strive for such concentration, the zealous effort motivated by that aspiration, and the results of that effort—great facility and perfect serenity.

The antidote for forgetting the object of meditation is recollection. The antidote for dullness and agitation is alertness.[63] The antidote for not applying the remedies to dullness and agitation is the mind which applies them.

The antidote for applying remedies when one is free from dullness and agitation is the equanimity of not applying (them). In order to eliminate the five impediments, I shall firmly rely on the application of these eight antidotes.

Hearing (the teachings), reflecting (upon their meaning), memory, alertness, effort and familiarity are the six forces.

Squeezing attention, interrupted attention, uninterrupted attention, and effortless attention are the four (types of attention).

(The nine mental stages are:) fixation, continuing fixation, patchlike fixation, close fixation, control, pacification, complete pacification, single-pointedness and meditative composure.

With the six forces, the four (types of) attention, and the nine mental stages, I will practise to achieve the bliss of great physical and mental facility and the perfect serene concentration resulting from that.[64]

(O Spiritual Masters), please bestow inspiring strength so that I may be able to do this.

The Way to Meditate upon Extraordinary Insight

After attaining perfect serene concentration I will continue to concentrate in that way, and then with thorough consideration I will carefully examine the meaning of self-existencelessness. Thus I will cut the root of (my) erring ignorance.

From beginningless time up to now, I and all other sentient beings have continuously wandered in cyclic existence, helplessly oppressed by innumerable sufferings. What is (the reason) for this?

Although the essence of the mind is neutral,[65] the attitude develops that self and others are independently self-existent. By the force of oneself and others appearing to be self-existent, there develops attachment for oneself, hatred for others, and all the other mental afflictions. With this (attitude) one accumulates deeds and thus circles in the six realms like a water wheel. In this way, upsetting waves of suffering arise.

Therefore, in the final analysis, this is the root of cyclic existence: all phenomena of cyclic existence and transcendence appear to be self-existent and are held to be (self-existent) without the understanding that (self-existence) is merely ascribed to them by conception.

Thus, the object to be refuted[66] is the "self" which appears to be a self-existent "I" rather than "I" ascribed to the assemblage of my body and mind.

If the "I" exists in the (self-existent) way that it appears to exist, then that (self-existent) "I" must be either identical with both the body and mind or separate from them, for there is no third way that it can exist.

If (there is a self-existent "I" that is) identical (with the body and mind), then just as the body and mind are two (entities), the "I" must also be two separate continuums. Or since the "I" is one (entity), both the body and mind must likewise be an indivisible whole.

Furthermore, if (there is a self-existent) "I" identical with the body and mind, then that must be one indistinguishable entity. The individual designations "my body" and "my mind" must therefore be incorrect.

For these and other reasons, there are many fallacies in (believing) that (there is a self-existent) "I" identical with the body and mind. Therefore, the self, or the "I," and both body and mind do not exist as one (self-existent) entity.

If one says that (there is a self-existent "I" that is) separate (from the body and mind), then they must be individual (entities). (Thus one must be able to say:) "This is the body; this is the mind; this is the 'I'." But since (three individual entities) do not exist like that, (a self-existent "I") does not exist separate (from the body and mind).

For these reasons, (a self-existent) "I" does not exist as either separate from or identical with body and mind. Rather, the "I," like an illusion, is not truly existent,[67] but comes from the assemblage of both body and mind.

Similarly, the "body" appears to be self-existent rather than merely ascribed to a heap of flesh and bones assembled into five limbs. This appearance of true (self-existence) is an object to be refuted.

If the body exists in the (self-existent) way that it appears to exist, then it must be either identical with or separate from the body's parts, since there is no other way that it can exist.

If (there is a self-existent body) identical (with the parts of the body) then since there are many parts of the body—the head and so forth—there must be many bodies as well. Or since there is one body, the many parts of the body must be an indivisible whole.

If (there is a self-existent body) separate (from the parts of the body), then when each of the body's parts—the arms, legs, etc.—are eliminated, one must say of what is left: "This is the body." But since there is nothing (left), the body also is merely ascribed to the assemblage of its parts.

(This same reasoning applies) also to the mind. (Take) Devadatta's mind (for example). That which appears to be self-existent, not merely ascribed to the earlier and later parts (of the continuum) of Devadatta's mind, is the way in which the object to be refuted appears.

If Devadatta's mind exists (self-existently) like that, then the mind must be either identical with or separate from its earlier and later parts, for there is no other way that it can exist.

If (Devadatta has a self-existent mind) identical (with its parts), then since there are many earlier and later parts of his mind, he must have many minds as well. Or just as his mind is one (entity), its earlier and later parts must be an indivisible whole.

(If Devadatta has a self-existent mind) separate (from its parts), then after eliminating all the parts which are earlier and later instances of his mind, one must be able to show his "mind" which is (self-existent). But since there is no (mind) that exists like that, "mind" is only ascribed to its earlier and later parts.

Thus, when the "I", the body, and the mind are examined with the points,[68] they are (understood to be) not intrinsically existent. Likewise, when all composite and non-composite phenomena are examined in that way, they are seen to be like space.[69]

In summary, all phenomena of cyclic existence and transcendence, without exception, are merely established by terms and conceptions. No phenomena, not even the tiniest atoms, exist on their own.

Well then, if all phenomena are not independently self-existent, then in what manner do they exist? They exist in a manner that is void of self-existence but appears (to be self-existent) like an illusion, a dream, an echo, and a moon in the water.

Even so, all phenomena are not utterly non-existent. An echo, for example, will occur when its causes assemble. And when (the echo) is examined, although (its self-existence) cannot be found, still (the echo) is not non-existent.

It is the same for all phenomena. When their interdependent (elements) assemble, and those (phenomena) and their appearances are examined by reasoning that investigates the absolute (truth), although nothing whatever (is found) to exist (self-existently), (the phenomena) are not utterly non-existent.

When something is examined (correctly), that which is seen as non-existent is seen as not truly (self-) existent but is not seen as utterly non-existent. It exists merely as ascription. Like an echo, only the true (self-) existence of its existence does not exist.

For that reason, when all phenomena are examined with reasoning that investigates their profound significance, they are seen to be like space, and even greater certainty is found that interdependence of action and result is valid. This is the ultimate of views.

(After realizing this, I must) cultivate the practice of (perceiving objects that appear in) post-meditation as illusions in the following way. Even when (a magician causes) illusory horses or bulls to appear in my sight, because I am certain that they do not exist, I understand the appearance to be an illusion.

Likewise, there is nothing wrong in knowing that all phenomena (exist merely as) ascriptions. By the force of having ascertained (during space-like meditation) that appearances are void of self-existence, one spontaneously perceives the objects appearing in post-meditation as illusions. There is no way other than this to meditate upon illusion.

I shall therefore combine the practice of spacelike meditation with the practice of (perceiving) the objects that appear in post-meditation as illusions. I shall attain the profound path combining extraordinary insight with perfect serene concentration that focuses upon the profound significance (of voidness).[70]

(O Spiritual Masters), please bestow inspiring strength so that I may be able to do this.

The Way to Enter the Vajra Vehicle

After actualizing the complementary paths of renunciation, Bodhi mind, and (correct) view, I shall (find) a fully qualified supreme Vajra master and please him with the three delights. Obtaining the four empowerments, I will plant seeds of the four bodies.[71] Exerting myself in the two stages of practice on the profound (Tantric) path, I will quickly achieve the state of unification.

(O Spiritual Masters), please bestow inspiring strength so that I may be able to do this.

Conclusion

Now recite the prayers (which conclude Jor Cho), beginning with:

> From the collection of both (merit and wisdom), as vast as
> space, accumulated through the effort I've made for so long
> in these (practices), may I become the chief of victorious
> leaders (for the sake of) all beings whose minds have been
> blinded by ignorance.

Then recite this concluding prayer:

Alas, (in all my) previous (lives), I have circled in cyclic existence like
a water wheel, most often wandering in places of no leisure without
meeting this excellent path.

In this (life) I have obtained a foundation of leisure and
endowments, am cared for by an excellent spiritual guide, and have
met the supreme path; to remain at ease now is extremely foolish.

Threfore, abandoning actions done (solely) for this life, just as a
snake sheds its skin, I shall strive day and night on this excellent path
and so make (this life) meaningful.

By the force of the virtue which I have created in this way, in all
my subsequent lives may I never be separated from the ways of Dharma
and may all beings be liberated through this path.

Author's Statement of Intention and Dedication

Thus, "the essence of nectar—the supreme Dharma, the way to practice profound instructions on the stages of the Bodhi path" has been
set forth in verses that (cover) the essential points and avoid complex
arrangement of the subject matter.

My name in Sanskrit is Jnana Virya. At the Ganden Samten Ling hermitage in Kong Yul, I, the lowest of Buddhist practitioners, composed this (text) with the intention of performing scanning meditation myself and also with the hope of benefitting others of similar fortune. (By virtue of) this, may the essence of (Buddha's) teachings become a banner of victory that will never vanish.

Notes

1. This verse is the full title of the text. The Tibetan is: *Byang chub lam ga'i rim pa'i gdams pa zab mo rnams tsigs su bcad pa'i sgo nas nyams su len tsul dam chos bdud rtz'i snying po zhes bya ba bzhugs so.* This text is also known in Tibetan by the shorter title *Lam rim bdud rtzi'i snying po*, which is translated as *The Essence of Nectar—The Stages of the Path.*

2. This verse accords with a standard rule of composition established for the following reason. Homage and going for refuge to the gurus is an effective method of collecting merit which, in general, is the basis for accomplishment of all goals up to Buddhahood and, in this case, helps the author to complete the text.

3. Visualize as actually existing before you in space the objects of refuge just as they are described in the text (also see frontispiece). The central object of refuge is your own Root Guru in the form of Buddha Shakyamuni. In Guru Shakyamuni's heart sits the holder of the vajra (a Buddha, deep blue in color, embracing his consort). This composite central figure is called "Spiritual Master—Lord of Sages—Holder of the Vajra." The bowl in his left hand contains nectar which acts as an antidote to the three poisons—greed, hatred and ignorance. His robes never touch him but remain about an inch from his luminous body.

   In the space surrounding him are the direct and lineage gurus. There are three major lineages. The lineage that bestows the inspiring strength of Tantric practice is behind him (pictured as above him in the frontispiece). The lineage of vast Bodhisattva conduct is at his right side (your left as you face him). The lineage of the profound view is at his left. Your own direct gurus are in front of him (pictured as slightly below him in the frontispiece). The Kadam lineage and the Ganden Kadam lineage are both in front of each of the three major lineages (pictured as part of the major lineages in the frontispiece), because they derive their tradition from all three. Below the Spiritual Master—Lord of Sages—Holder of the

Vajra, in seven successive rows forming the shape of a tree are (from top to bottom): Tantric deities, Buddhas, Bodhisattvas, hearkeners, solitary victors, heroes and celestials, and Dharma protectors. All the objects of refuge have the white letter *om* on their foreheads, the red letter *ah* on their throats, and the blue letter *hum* on their hearts. Beams of colored light radiate from all these letters and wherever they strike, whatever is needed to bring sentient beings to spiritual maturity appears.

All sentient beings surround you. Although these beings are experiencing the various sufferings of the six realms, they appear to be human in form so that you can relate to them. The female beings and your mother are on your left, the male beings and your father are on your right, and you are in the centre. After developing sufficient motivation, all the sentient beings, with you as their leader, take refuge.

After you all take refuge, streams of luminous ambrosia flow from the objects of refuge through the tops of your heads. All your non-virtues, obstructions, physical ailments, and so forth appear as thick, black liquid and poisonous insects inside your bodies. As the luminous ambrosia flows in, the black liquid and insects flow out through your lower orifices into crevices in the earth where the Lord of Death, with mouth wide open, swallows them and becomes satiated. Your bodies become completely filled with luminous ambrosia and you acquire all the qualities of the Buddha.

4. Visualize that countless identical fields of the accumulation of merit, each one complete with all the objects of refuge, appear and then dissolve into the original field like snowflakes falling into water. You should now feel that this field of the accumulation of merit is the combination of all objects of refuge and that its great qualities of wisdom, compassion, power, dignity, and so forth are thereby increased.

5. In order to achieve Buddhahood by relying solely upon the vehicle of the six perfections, you must accumulate merit and wisdom for three immeasurable eons. By properly practising Tantra, however, you can achieve the state of unification (Buddhahood) in one lifetime which by comparison is only an instant.

6. The eight traditional outer offerings are: ambrosia for drinking, water for bathing, flowers, incense, light, perfumed water for sprinkling on the body, fine food, and music. Other outer offerings are: offerings to the five senses, various types of wealth and good fortune, things owned by oneself and others, and ownerless things (forests, oceans, beautiful views, etc.). Inner offerings include all of one's virtues, and so on. Actually present whatever offerings you can and visualize the rest; through

visualization increase them in quality and number to pervade all of space. As you make the eight outer offerings, you should consider them as representing inner offerings in the following way. Hearing, contemplating and meditating upon the teachings of Sutra and Tantra are like a vast lake of nectar for drinking and bathing, in which flowers of good qualities grow. These flowers emit the wonderful fragrance of morality. Wisdom is the light by which all things are perceived and understood; the three types of faith are perfumed water; concentration is the finest food (when eaten it increases, when not eaten it decreases); chanting praises to the good qualities of the supreme objects of refuge is the most beautiful music.

The two types of offerings not made at the beginning stages of practice are offerings of voidness and Tantric offerings.

7. All levels of the bodhi path—the hearkener, solitary victor and Bodhisattva stages, solitary liberation and Buddhahood—are worthy goals and you may request success in any or all of the practices aimed at them. For example, a person of small scope requests protection from unfortunate rebirths; a person of intermediate scope requests success in the three trainings and the attainment of solitary liberation; a person of great scope requests success in practising the six perfections, adherence to Bodhisattva vows, and attainment of Buddhahood. You should also request success in the specific practices that you are presently engaged in.

8. Confession of your non-virtuous deeds is necessary in order to conteract their causal force which, if allowed to mature, will bring you suffering. There are four forces which provide an effective antidote:

    i.   Because the objects of your erroneous deeds are the Three Jewels, whose precepts you have transgressed, and sentient beings, whom you have harmed, you should take refuge and develop bodhi mind.

    ii. Sincerely regret your erroneous deeds by realizing their consequences.

    iii. Develop the conviction never to repeat them.

    iv. Apply specific antidotes such as patience for anger, generosity for stinginess, etc., and engage in virtuous activities such as the seven limbs, recitation of mantras and texts (e.g., *The Confession of Moral Downfalls, The Heart Sutra*), and, best of all, meditate on voidness.

9. Rejoicing is the easiest way to collect merit and one of the most effective. The amount of merit acquired depends upon your own level of spiritual development and upon the level of the object of your rejoicing. For example, you will acquire more merit by rejoicing in the deeds of a Bodhisattva than in the deeds of an ordinary being. A Bodhisattva will acquire more merit

than an ordinary person when both rejoice in the same object. It is also beneficial to rejoice in your own virtuous actions.

10. Requesting teachings is necessary, for without being asked the gurus will not give instructions, and a practitioner who has not heard oral instructions from the gurus of an unbroken lineage is like an armless rock climber.

   At this point it is auspicious to visualize a golden wheel and offer it to the objects of refuge while requesting teachings. This practice stems from the offering of a golden wheel by Brahma and Indra to Buddha Shakyamuni when he first taught Dharma after attaining Buddhahood.

11. Beseeching your gurus to live a long life is an important practice, for they may pass away if there is not a manifest need for them to remain in order to teach and empower their disciples. Not only does this practice increase their lifespan, it also increases yours.

12. Dedicating the merit of your virtuous actions is essential because great accumulations of merit are instantly destroyed by anger and other mental afflictions, but merit which has been dedicated to the attainment of supreme bodhi can never be fully destroyed from the roots as it can when dedicated to other goals. The force of dedication to other goals is exhausted when those goals are attained, but the force of dedication to the attainment of supreme bodhi will never be exhausted, because even after you have attained Buddhahood, the fruit of that will continue to increase through your Buddha activity for sentient beings.

13. Offering a mandala is symbolic of offering the entire purified universe to the objects of refuge. There are various mandala offerings with recitations and you may do the one of your choice. A short mandala offering is as follows:

   The earth covered with incense and strewn with flowers,
   Mount Meru adorned by the four continents, sun and moon,

   I visualize as a Buddha land and offer (to you, O objects of refuge)
   So that all sentient beings may live in a pure realm.
   Idam Guru Ratna Mandalakam Niryatayami.
   I send forth this mandala to you, precious gurus.

When reciting the next seven verses of the text, repeat the request which comes at the end of each verse. (Note—except in the first verse these requests read: "please bestow inspiring strength on the continuum of my mind.") Visualize that your Root Guru is above your head and that you are both making requests—he on your behalf—to the Spiritual Master

—Lord of Sages—Holder of the Vajra, who is in the centre of the field of the accumulation of merit. As you first make each request, multicolored luminous beams of nectar stream from his body and the bodies of all the objects of refuge through the top of your head and into your body. The luminous nectar instantly dispels all your non-virtue, mental afflictions, physical ailments, and so forth, which are in the form of darkness, just as a light when turned on in a dark room instantly dispels the darkness there. As you repeat the request, the luminous wisdom nectar fills your body, replacing the darkness with all the physical and mental qualities of a Buddha and increasing your lifespan as well.

For this and all the previous practices in this text (the seven limbs, other visualizations, etc.), it is very important to have the strong conviction that what you have visualized has really occurred and that your requests have been granted. In this case, for instance, you should firmly believe that you have been transformed into a Buddha by the blessings of your gurus. Although at this time you may not actually receive such attainment through this practice, powerful instincts or seeds are planted in your mental continuum. These seeds are nurtured by the inspiring strength you receive from your Guru and when they come to maturity, you achieve the ultimate goal.

14. This request, used in Tantra, refers to your attainment of Unification (Buddhahood), the stage at which your body, speech and mental continuum reach perfection and thus acquire the qualities of your Root Guru and all other Buddhas.

15. Up to this point, preparations for meditation on the stages of the path have been made. The following verses are requests for success in practicing each stage: guru devotion (1st verse), the path in common with a person of small scope (verses 2-5), the path in common with a person of intermediate scope (verses 6-8), the development of wishing bodhi mind (verses 9-10), participating bodhi mind—especially the six perfections (verse 11), special request concerning the perfection of deep concentration (verse 12) and concerning the perfection of wisdom (verse 13). After requests are completed, instructions for meditating on these stages begin.

16. Before engaging in this practice it is necessary to find a properly qualified guru. There are different qualifications for a teacher of the small vehicle, a spiritual guide of the great vehicle, and a Tantric master. To follow the path outlined in this text you must determine by careful examination that the person you choose for a guru has the qualities of a spiritual guide of the great vehicle. As enumerated in the *Mahayana*

Sutralankara of Maitreya, there are ten: a mental continuum subdued by morality, pacification of mental distractions by concentration, elimination of grasping at self-existence by wisdom, qualities superior to the disciple's, correct realization of the actual nature of phenomena (either directly or conceptually) through the wisdom of hearing, skill in teaching, a compassionate nature, and unflagging enthusiasm. At the very least, he must have: amental continuum subdued by the three trainings (extraordinary morality, concentration and wisdom), compassion, and realization of the actual nature of phenomena through the many teachings he has heard.

17. White deeds refer to virtuous deeds and bring only happiness. Black deeds refer to non-virtuous deeds and bring only suffering.

18. At first, the meditator comes to separate realizations of absolute truth (the voidness of self-existence) and relative truth (the appearance of interdependent origination). Then his two realizations become stronger as he alternates between them. Finally, when he attains Buddhahood, he perceives the two truths simultaneously.

19. You cannot successfully practise Tantra without empowerment. At the time of empowerment, the initiate takes serious vows which if broken and not counteracted produce the mature result of rebirth in the lowest hell, and even if counteracted still carry serious consequences. For empowerment to be effective, the initiate must receive it from a qualified Vajra guru who has received it himself from a valid, unbroken lineage (i.e., from a succession of Tantric masters originating with Buddha Vajradhara). The Vajra guru must also have completed a meditational retreat of the deity including a "fire puja". In addition he should make sure that the initiates are qualified. Understanding the stages of the path and the initiation itself are the minimum prerequisites for initiates.

20. The state of unification is attained when the developing and fulfilment stages of Tantra are mastered. During these stages two major obstacles are abandoned: ordinary appearances and attraction to ordinary appearances. It is then that the world appears as a pure realm and the inhabitants appear as deities.

21. The bodhi path, in general, may be divided into three types each having five paths: (1) the five progressive paths of a hearkener ending at solitary liberation; (ii) the five progressive paths of a solitary victor ending at solitary liberation; and (iii) the five progressive paths of the great vehicle ending at omniscient Buddhahood. While progressing through the paths of the great vehicle a Bodhisattva passes through ten levels beginning with his direct insight into absolute truth and ending with his imminent attainment of Buddhahood.

22. Every deed produces four types of result:

    i. a matured result
    ii. experience in accordance with the cause
    iii. activity in accordance with the cause

    iv. results in common with other beings.

    As the results of devotion to a spiritual master, for example, you will:

    i. attain the states of definite goodness
    ii. meet with a spiritual master in future lives
    iii. be properly devoted to him in future lives
    iv. live in a land where Spiritual Masters teach the Dharma

23. The Buddha emanates in whatever form is suited for the development of individual beings Thus, for an Exalted Bodhisattva he may appear as the Body of Utility, whereas for an ordinary being without such spiritual development, he may appear as a Spiritual Guide, a monk, a ruler, a servant, or even as a tree or a bridge. Only those whose previous deeds have created the necessary cause can be present when he appears as a World Teacher like Sakyamuni Buddha or Maitreya Buddha.

24. Devadatta was Buddha Sakymuni's envious younger brother (or cousin) who thought himself superior to Buddha. Bhiksu Leg Par Gar Ma was a contemporary of Buddha who claimed to see only a halo and numerous faults as Buddha's attributes. There were also many philosophers who believed Buddha's teachings to be defective.

25. Entering the religious life is generally thought to mean taking the ordination of a monk or nun. But whether or not you are ordained, your motivation, practice and accomplishments are the true measure of religious life. When you are no longer attached to the pleasures of cyclic existence, you have left secular life. When your mind is no longer distracted by appearances, you are dwelling in seclusion.

26. As a human you are able to create the necessary karma to be reborn in a pure realm rather than in cyclic existence. There are even methods by which many famous practitioners have passed on to pure realms without changing from their human form.

27. This refers to the anecdote about a lame man called Gru-gu. One day he fell asleep while sitting on the edge of a precipice. He fell off and landed on the back of a wild ass grazing on a ledge a short distance below, and as he rode the animal to safety he began to sing. When other herdsmen saw this they asked him why. He replied, "By incredible good fortune, I was saved today from falling to my death, and now I, a lame man, am riding a wild ass which even you cannot do. What has happened can never happen again. When will I sing with joy if not now?"

28. The Lord of Death is symbolically represented as a demon but is not an external power at all. In actuality, the Lord of Death is the force of your own deeds and mental afflictions which cause you to be born and to die without control.

29. The lifespan of human beings at the beginning of an eon is immeasurable but gradually diminishes until it reaches a limit of ten years. Then, the average lifespan gradually begins to increase again. At this time, the average lifespan is less than one hundred years with no certainty of even lasting that long.

30. There are two Wailing Hells. The more severe of the two is called the Great Wailing Hell and its suffering is double that of the first.

31. You may rely on the help of others in ordinary matters but never rely on anything other than the Three Jewels to help you gain liberation from cyclic existence.

32. Conviction, the strongest type of faith, is based on clear understanding. You should therefore understand the relationship between deeds and results, the area of cause and effect that deals with actions of sentient beings.

33. Mindfulness has two functions: cherishing virtuous mental activities and deeds, and protecting the mind from mental afflictions and the causes of mental afflictions. Alertness keeps watch to see that the mind does not stray from virtuous objects. Memory brings the mind back to its mindfulness of virtue when it goes astray.

34. By illustration, it is impossible for a wheat sprout to grow without a seed or from a barley seed, because without a seed there is no cause for a wheat sprout to grow and a barley seed does not provide a suitable cause.

35. The force of a deed is never lost. If not counteracted it will produce a result when the appropriate conditions assemble, no matter how long that may take.

36. See note no. 8.

37. Anger instantly destroys vast accumulationsof merit (note no. 12). A single moment of anger in one Bodhisattva towards another, for instance, can destroy the merit he has accumulated during a hundred eons. Wrong views, such as those concerning deeds and results, have an even greater force of destruction for they cut off virtues at the very root. In contrast to this, refraining from anger (i.e., patience), developing conviction and mindfulness about deeds and results, etc., bring great merit.

38. The preceding teachings are for people of small, intermediate and great scope. In this section, teachings in common for people of intermediate and

great scope are given, followed by teachings exclusively for those of great scope. As with a cat, horse and elephant, the larger animals can carry the loads of smaller animals but not vice versa. The goal to which you aspire determines what you practise, and what you practise determines your ability (See note no. 7). This is what is meant by "scope".

39. A fetus experiences suffering when its mother eats food that is too hot, cold or spicy and engages in actions that are too strenuous or abrupt, such as running, jumping, having sexual intercourse, etc.

40. According to the Tibetan medical system, physical illnesses are related to imbalances in the four elements that comprise the body—earth, air, fire and water. These physical elements are interrelated with mental factors.

41. At the time of death, your bodily functions dissipate as the physical elements "dissolve". At that time various painful and fearsome halluci-nations may be experienced by the dying person, such as falling off a precipice, being swept along by a swift river or a great wave, burning up, sinking, and so forth.

42. The matured results of demigods' past deeds have brought them wealth and so forth, but because of these pleasures, they have no wish to renounce cyclic existence and thus they lack motivation to practice Dharma.

43. Throughout their lives the gods have bodies. clothes, garlands, etc., that remain perfectly fresh. Then a week before their death, they begin to sweat, their clothes become smelly and worn, their flower garlands wither, their lounges become uncomfortable, and so forth; these are called the signs of approaching death. As the gods die, they experience dissolving of the elements as humans do; these are called the symptoms of impending death (see note no. 41).

44. When the signs of approaching death occur, the gods are unable to enjoy their previous pleasures, their friends avoid them, and they go off to spend their remaining time in isolation. With clairvoyance they unhappily see where they will be reborn. This suffering lasts for a long duration because "one week" for the lowest level gods is 350 human years.

45. The three realms of cyclic existence are the desire, form, and formless realms. Gods live in the upper regions of the desire realm and the two realms above that—the form and formless. Whereas six types of beings live in the desire realm, only higher level gods live in the form and formless realms.

46. Any being who uncontrollably takes birth by the force of deeds and mental afflictions is subject to the suffering of conditional existence. This pervasive

suffering is as difficult for you to feel as a hair in the palm of your hand. For others with more sensitivity however, this suffering is like a hair in the eye.

47. Up to this point, the specific sufferings of each realm have been presented. This section shows the six general sufferings of cyclic existence: i) relinquishing the body after each life, (ii) the changing nature of friends and enemies, (iii) insecurity in status and wealth, (iv) the inability of companions and friends to really help, (v) dissatisfaction, and (vi) recurrent, uncertain rebirth.

48. In Buddhist metaphysics, the sun, moon and stars are regarded as beings. The orbs of the sun, moon and stars are regarded as the dwelling place of those beings.

49. All sufferings may be classified into three types: (i) the suffering of misery, which includes all unpleasant experiences; (ii) the suffering of change, which includes pleasant experiences that come to an end because they are contaminated; (iii) the suffering of conditional existence (see note no. 46).

50. "Contaminated" refers to anything that arises from deeds and mental afflictions, and thus is encompassed by any of the three types of suffering.

51. There are five aggregates: form, feeling, cognition, the (other mental) compositional factors, and consciousness.

52. The contaminated aggregates are like water, and suffering is like the bubbles that invariably arise in it. Both have the same nature: only their forms are different.

53. These teachings tame the mind of a person of intermediate scope. They are like medicine to cure the disease of cyclic existence. Je Tsong Ka Pa said that we will not even wish to renounce cyclic existence unless we contemplate its faults, and that we will not be able to achieve the cessation of our suffering unless we recognize the cause of cyclic existence and cut it at the root.

54. Grasping at self-existence is a being's distorted perception of himself and other phenomena as independent and self-existent. This erroneous view is the root of all non-virtuous thoughts, actions and results.

55. The wisdom of realizing self-existencelessness is direct realization of the non-self-existence of oneself and all other phenomena; i.e., it is perception of absolute truth.

56. There are four types of birth. The two that do not require parents are: (i) birth in warmth and moisture, and (ii) miraculous birth. The two that do require parents are: (iii) birth from an egg, and (iv) birth from a womb.

57. The sphere of Dharma is a synonym for voidness. Only the Buddha can meditate on voidness and relative phenomena simultaneously.

58. The preceding method of meditation beginning with "The way to practice mental equilibrium" is called: "Seven Instructions of Cause and Result." It was taught by Maitreya to Asanga and passed down through Atisha. The first six parts are causes for the seventh, the development of bodhi mind. The following method is called: "Equalizing and Exchanging Self and Others." It was taught by Manjushri to Nagarjuna and passed down through Shantideva and then Atisha. Je Tsong Khapa taught the combination of these two methods as the most effective way to develop bodhi mind.

59. The wish to experience the results of others' evil deeds so that they will not suffer is an expression of pure compassion. The wish for them to experience the results of your own good deeds so that they will have happiness is an expression of pure love. The preceding meditations lead to those wishes.

60. According to the Madhyamika school, transcendental concentration refers to the deep concentration possessed by those who directly perceive the voidness of self-existence. According to the other schools of Buddhism, it refers to the deep concentration possessed by those who have transcended cyclic existence. Mundane concentration refers to the deep concentration possessed by those without such attainments.

61. There are four correct views:

   i. All composite phenomena are impermanent.

   ii. All contaminated phenomena are suffering.

   iii. The transcendence of cyclic existence is liberation.

   iv. All phenomena are void of independent self-existence.

   The correct view referred to in this verse is the fourth one, which is the highest.

62. In developing perfect serene concentration, any object may be chosen to focus upon, but once chosen it should not be changed until perfect serenity is achieved.

63. Alertness is not actually the main antidote for dullness and agitation. Alertness or vigilance is like a guard that warns when dullness and agitation endanger meditation. The main opponents are the specific antidotes that the meditator applies to the various stages of coarse and subtle dullness and agitation. You should receive detailed instructions from a qualified teacher about the specific antidotes and the other elements involved in perfect serenity meditation if you intend to engage in this practice.

64. The nine mental stages are progressive levels of increasing concentration that are passed through in the practice of perfect serenity meditation. The meditator employs six forces to help him advance through these stages and he experiences four types of attention while meditating. After achieving the ninth mental stage he develops the bliss of great mental and physical facility. He then goes on to attain perfect serene concentration.

65. The mind itself is neutral: i.e., neither virtuous nor non-virtuous. When it becomes associated with either virtue or non-virtue, however, it temporarily takes on that characteristic.

66. "The object to be refuted" may be any object whose existence is negated by valid logic.

67. "Not truly existent" means that phenomena do not truly exist as they appear to ordinary beings; i.e., they are not truly self-existent. A synonym for this is "voidness" which means void of self-existence.

68. The four points are:
    i.   Recognizing the object to be refuted.
    ii. Understanding its implications.
    iii. Realizing that it does not exist as a single (self-existent entity).
    iv. Realizing that it does not exist as many (self-existent entities).

69. Space is neither one nor many self-existent entities; it exists only by ascription. Likewise, the same is true for the "I", the body, the mind and all phenomena. In a metaphorical sense, just as space is void of obstructions, the "I", the body, the mind and all phenomena are empty of self-existence.

70. One "combines" these meditations by alternating them. Only a Buddha can meditate on absolute and relative truth simultaneously; only he can perceive the voidness and interdependent origination of phenomena at the same time.

71. The various paths set forth in the Sutras are not in the least contrary to one another or to the practices of Tantra. All of them are complementary. In fact, before starting to practise Tantra, you must first engage in all the stages from guru devotion to meditation on voidness, especially the three main practices—renunciation, bodhi mind, and understanding of voidness. Then you may receive the four seed initiations which empower you to perform Tantric meditations. These empowerments plant seeds in your mental continuum which eventually ripen in your attainment of the four bodies of a Buddha.

Glossary

The words in parenthesis following glossary terms are the transliteration of Tibetan spelling as it appeared in the text, sometimes followed by its Sanskrit equivalent. (Note: the Sanskrit letter "s" is pronounced "sh")

ABSOLUTE TRUTH *(don-dam bden-pa)*. Synonyms are correct view, fundamental true nature, not truly existent, self-existencelessness, sphere of Dharma, true nature, voidness, void of self-existence.

ADHERENCE *(dam-tsig; samaya)*. The keeping of one's vows and commitments. Sometimes used as a synonym of vows and commitments.

AGITATION *(rgod-pa)*. Coarse agitation is the mind partially focusing on any object other than the object of meditation. Subtle agitation is the feeling of "highness" which distracts one during meditation.

AIR *(rlung)*. One of the four elements.

ALERTNESS *(shes-bzhin)*. See notes no. 33 and no. 63.

ARHAT *(dgra-bcom-pa, arhat)*. Literally, foe vanquisher. There are three types: (1) one who has attained liberation from cyclic existence as a hearkener, (2) as a solitary victor, or (3) one who has attained Buddhahood.

ASCRIBED *(btags-pa)*. Established by terms and conception.

ASCRIPTION *(tha-nyad)*. Conventional existence; term and conception.

ATISHA *(a-ti-sha; Atisha)*. A great Buddhist pandit from India who brought the three major lineages to Tibet (982-1054).

BILLION WORLDS *(zhing-stong-gsum)*. A thousand times a thousand times a thousand worlds, each with a Brahma heaven at its highest point.

BLISTERING HELL *(chu-bu-can)*. First of the eight cold hells.

BODHI *(byang-chub; bodhi)*. In Tibetan, the first syllable signifies the elimination of erroneous deeds and obstructions; the second syllable signifies the acquisition of merit and wisdom. There are three types: the bodhi of hearkeners, solitary victors and Buddhas. The bodhi of hearkeners and solitary victors includes the elimination of erroneous deeds and mental afflictions (but not the obstructions to omniscience) and the attainment of solitary liberation from cyclic existence. The Bodhi of Buddhas includes the elimination of all obstructions and the attainment of omniscient Buddhahood.

BODHI MIND *(byang-chub-kyi sems; bodhicitta).* Absolute bodhi mind is the direct perception of absolute truth by an exalted one of the great vehicle. Relative bodhi mind is distinguished into wishing and participating. Wishing bodhi mind is the wish to attain Buddhahood in order to liberate all sentient beings from cyclic existence. Participating bodhi mind is involvement in the Bodhisattva vows and practises.

BODHI PATH *(byang-chub-lam).* See note no. 21.

BODHISATTVA *(byang-chub sems-dpa'; bodhisattva).* One who has entered the paths of the great vehicle.

BODHISATTVA CONDUCT *(byang-chub sems-dpa'i spyod-pa).* The six perfections and the four ways of gathering disciples. Synonyms: Bodhisattva practises, Bodhisattva activities.

BODHISATTVA VOWS *(byang-sdom, or byang-sems-kyi sdom-pa).* The eighteen major and forty-six minor vows that one takes in participating bodhi mind.

BODY OF DHARMA *(chos-sku; Dharmakaya).* The Buddha's mind which includes the body of dharma nature and the body of dharma knowledge.

BODY OF DHARMA KNOWLEDGE *(ye-shes chos-sku; Jnana- dharmakaya).* The Buddha's omniscience.

BODY OF DHARMA NATURE *(ngo-bo nyid-sku; Svabha- vikakaya).* The voidness of Buddha's mind.

BODY OF FORM *(gzugs-sku; Rupakaya).* Includes the Body of utility and the body of physical manifestation.

BODY OF PHYSICAL MANIFESTATION *(sprul-sku; Nirmana-kaya).* All physical manifestations of Buddha other than the body of utility. See note no. 23.

BODY OF UTILITY *(longs-sku, Sambhogakaya).* The form of Buddha with five definite attributes: exists in the pure realm of Og Min, exists until cyclic existence ends, surrounded only by exalted Bodhisattva disciples, gives only teachings of the great vehicle, and possesses the 112 marks of perfection.

BRAHMA *(tsangs-pa; Brahma)*. A god in cyclic existence.

BUDDHA *(sangs-rgyas; Buddha)*. One who has eliminated all obstructions and attained omniscience, Synonyms: Arhat of the Great Vehicle, Conqueror, Lord of Sages, Master Teacher, Omniscient One, One Who Has Gone To Suchness, Victorious One, Victorious Lord, etc.

BUDDHA SHAKYAMUNI *(sha'-kya thub-pa; Shakyamuni)*. Literally, Sage of the Shakya (family). This is an epithet of Gautama Buddha, the fourth world teacher of this eon.

BUDDHAHOOD *(sangs-rgyas-kyi go-'phang)*. The state of a Buddha. See BUDDHA, BODHI.

CELESTIALS *(mkha'-'gro; dakini)*. A type of goddess that helps Tantric practitioners. Some live in cyclic existence, some in pure realms. In the field of the accumulation of merit they are emanations of Buddha.

CESSATION *('gog-pa)*. May refer to the partial or complete cessation of erroneous deeds and obstructions.

COMPASSION *(snying-rje; karuna)*. The wish for others to be free from suffering.

COMPOSITE *('dus-byas; samskrita)*

CONCENTRATION *(ting-'dzin, or ting-nge-dzin; samadhi)*. The many types of concentration include: ordinary, deep, single-pointed, and perfect serene.

CONFESSION OF MORAL DOWNFALLS *(ltung-bshags)*. A text to be recited for counteracting non-virtuous deeds.

CONQUEROR *(bcom-ldan-'das; bhagavan)*. An epithet of Buddha. See BUDDHA.

CONTAMINATED *(zag-bcas)*. See note no. 50.

CONTAMINATED AGGREGATES *(nyer-lan phung-po)*. See notes nos. 50, 51, 52.

CORRECT VIEW *(yang-dag lta-ba)*. See note no. 61; see ABSOLUTE TRUTH.

CYCLIC EXISTENCE *(srid-pa or 'khor-ba; samsara)*. The continuous cycle of contaminated rebirths in the desire, form and formless realms.

DARK EON *(mun-bskal)*. The first half of each eon during which the average lifespan of beings is increasing. This time of increasing happiness is not conducive to the practise of Dharma and so Buddhas do not appear. Thus it is known as a time of darkness.

DE LAM *(bde-lam)*. A text on the stages of the path written by Panchen Losang Cho Gyan.

DEEDS *(las; karma)*. The actions of any sentient being. Deeds may be distinguished into two types: mental deeds—the activity associated with bringing consciousness to its object of attention, and instigated deeds—the activities of body and speech, which are brought about by the mind. Deeds are good, bad or neutral depending on their motivation and the mental factors with which they are associated. Virtuous deeds only result in happiness, non-virtuous deeds in suffering.

DEEP CONCENTRATION *(bsam-gtan; dhyana)*. A type of concentration. When associated with bodhi mind, it is the fifth of the six perfections. When associated with worldly motivation, it is a cause of rebirth as a samsaric god in the form or formless realms.

DEFINITE GOODNESS *(nges-legs)*. The states of solitary liberation and Buddhahood.

DELUDED VIEWS *(log-lta)*. Various wrong views such as eternalism, nihilism, the belief in one's own self-existence, and disbelief in Buddha's teachings on cause and results, the path, liberation, etc.

DHARMA *(chos; dharma)*. May mean "phenomena" or "precious supreme dharma".

DHARMA PROTECTORS *(chos-srung; dharmagupta or chos-skyong; dharmapala)*. Non-samsaric beings who have vowed to protect the precious supreme Dharma and the practitioners of Dharma.

DIRECT GURUS *(dngos-kyi bla-ma)*. One's actual spiritual masters in this life.

DROMTONPA *('Brom-ston-pa)*. Chief disciple of Atisha.

DUAL GOAL *(don-gnyis)*. See ULTIMATE BENEFIT FOR SELF AND OTHERS.

DULLNESS *(bying-ba)*. Coarse dullness is mental and physical sluggishness and unclear focusing of mind upon the object of meditation. Subtle dullness is slight unclarity and weakness in focusing and is difficult to detect. See note no. 63.

EFFORT *(brtzon-'grus; virya)*. Fourth of the six perfections. Enthusiasm and perseverance in the practise of virtue.

EIGHT AUSPICIOUS SIGNS *(rtags-rdzas-brgyad, or bkra-shis rtags-brgyad)*. Precious umbrella, golden fish, inexhaustible treasure vase, good lotus, white conch shell with clockwise helix, glorious interwoven knot, supreme banner of victory, and golden wheel. These eight symbols are said to appear naturally in the ground of pure realms.

EIGHT MATURED ADVANTAGES *(rnam-smin yon-tan-brgyad)*. These advantages are the matured results of previously accumulated causes and provide favorable conditions for humans to practise Dharma. The eight are: long life, pleasing appearance, high birth, wealth, truthfulness, power and renown, mental and physical health and ability, and strong willpower.

EIGHTEEN FACTORS OF LEISURE AND ENDOWMENTS *(tal dang 'byor-ba-yi chos-bco-brgyad)*. The eight factors of leisure and ten endowments which enable one to practise Dharma. See LEISURE, ENDOWMENTS.

ELEVEN WAYS TO BENEFIT SENTIENT BEINGS *(sems-can don-byed rnam-pa bcu-gcig)*. (1) Alleviating their suffering, (2) alleviating their ignorance of Dharma, (3) repaying their kindness, (4) protecting them from danger and fear, (5) helping them overcome their mental misery and depression, (6) helping those who are destitute, (7) helping those who are homeless, (8) teaching and advising them according to their needs, (9) helping those on the wrong path, (10) encouraging those on the right path, (11) helping them with one's merit and supernormal powers.

EMANATIONS *(sprul-pa; nirmana)*. The supernormal manifestation of beings and forms. See note no. 23).

EMPOWERMENT *(dbang)*. Initiation into Tantra.

ENDOWMENTS *('byor-ba)*. There are ten endowments which enable one to practise Dharma: (1) birth as a human being, (2) birth in a "central country" where the opportunity to practise Dharma exists, (3) complete unimpaired faculties of body and mind, (4) a life without extremely perverted deeds, (5) faith in the teachings of Buddha, (6) advent of a Buddha or his representative—a qualified spiritual master—during one's lifetime, (7) his teaching of the Dharma, (8) the flourishing of the Dharma, (9) the existence of true followers of the Dharma, (10) the existence of favorable conditions for practise—especially the kindness of others. The first five endowments are personal and the latter five are circumstantial.

EQUILIBRIUM *(brtang-snyoms)*. The state of mind free from attachment, hatred and indifference towards sentient beings. Synonyms: equanimity, mental equilibrium.

ERRONEOUS DEEDS *(nyes-pa)*. Deeds which are associated with the mental afflictions and bring unhappiness as their result. See NATURAL NON-VIRTUES.

ETERNALISM *(rtag-pa'i lta-ba)*. The false view which holds all phenomena to be self-existent and believes in the existence of an eternal "self".

EVIL *(sdig-pa)*. See NATURAL NON-VIRTUES.

EXALTED ONE *('phags-pa; arya)*. Refers to any being who has reached the paths of insight; i.e. one who has directly perceived the absolute truth.

EXALTED ASSEMBLY *('phags-pa'i-tsogs)*. Synonym of Sangha. See EXALTED ONE, EXALTED SANGHA.

EXALTED SANGHA *('phags-pa'i dge-'dun; Arya Sangha)*. The community of exalted ones, one of the Three Jewels.

EXTRAORDINARY ATTITUDE *(lhag-bsam)*. The intention to liberate all sentient beings through one's own effort.

EXTRAORDINARY INSIGHT *(lhag-mthong; vipasyana)*.

EXTRAORDINARY MORALITY *(lhag-pa'i tsul-khrims; adhisila)*. One of the three trainings.

EXTRAORDINARY WISDOM *(lhag-pa'i shes-rab; adhiprajna)*. One of the three trainings.

FACILITY. See GREAT FACILITY.

FIELD OF THE ACCUMULATION OF MERIT *(tsogs-zhing)*. The Buddhist objects of refuge. See note no. 3.

FIVE DEGENERATIONS *(snyings-lgna)*. Decreasing lifespan, increasing wrong views, increasing mental afflictions, increasing difficulty in taming beings and increasing strife.

FIVE HEINOUS DEEDS *(mtsams-med lnga)*. Literally, the five (deeds which bring suffering) without respite (in the lowest of hells). The five are: killing one's mother, father or an arhat, causing schism in the Sangha, and causing injury to a Buddha.

FIVE LIMBS *(yan-lag-lnga)*. The entire body divided into five parts: the head, two arms and two legs.

FIVE SUBJECTS *(gnas-lnga, or rig-gnas-lnga)*. A great Buddhist pandit masters five major and five minor subjects. The five major are: (1) advanced medicine, (2) the making of mandalas, thangkas, stupas, etc., (3) advanced linguistics, (4) dialectics, and (5) Buddhist philosophy and religion. The five minor are: (1) basic medicine, (2) astrology, (3) semantics, (4) composition, and (5) poetry.

FORM AND FORMLESS REALMS *(gzugs dang gzugs-med-pa'i khams; rupadhatu and arupadhatu)*. See THREE REALMS.

FORTUNATE EON *(bskal-bzang; bhadrakalpa)*. See TIME OF LIGHT.

FOUR BODIES *(sku-bzhi)*. (1) The body of Dharma nature, (2) the body of Dharma knowledge, (3) the body of utility, (4) the body of physical manifestation.

FOUR CONTINENTS *(gling-bzhi)*. The eastern, southern, western and northern continents of the world as visualized in the mandala offering.

FOUR DOORS THROUGH WHICH MORAL DOWNFALLS OCCUR *(ltung-ba 'byung-ba'i sgo-bzhi).* Not knowing what is right and wrong, carelessness in one's thoughts and actions, possessing numerous mental afflictions, and lacking respect for the teachings of Buddha.

FOUR ELEMENTS *('byung-pa'i bzhi).* Earth, air, fire and water.

FOUR EMPOWERMENTS *(dbang-bzhi).* The four seed initiations of Tantra. See note no. 71.

FOUR FORCES *(stobs-bzhi).* The forces for counteracting non-virtuous actions. See note no. 8. Synonym: purifying forces.

FOUR IMMEASURABLES *(tsad-med-bzhi).* (1) Immeasurable equanimity, (2) immeasurable loving kindness, (3) immeasurable compassion, and (4) immeasurable joy.

FOUR POINTS *(gnad-bzhi).* The four points of analysis for understanding voidness. See note no. 68.

FUNDAMENTAL TRUE NATURE *(gdod-ma'i gnas-lugs).* See ABSOLUTE TRUTH.

GANDEN KADAM LINEAGE *(dga'-ldan bka'-brgyud).* Literally, the lineage (stemming from) Ganden (Monastery) that gives instructions on (Buddha's) speech. This lineage is a continuation of the Kadam lineage combined with teachings from the other major lineages in Tibet. It was organized by Je Tsong Khapa who founded Ganden Monastery. This lineage is usually called the Gelugpa lineage.

GENTLE GURU PROTECTOR *('jam-mgon bla-ma).* Epithet of Je Tsong Khapa.

GOING FOR REFUGE *(skyabs-su-mchi, or skyabs-'gro).* Going for refuge is the attitude of looking for help. Extraordinary going for refuge is looking to the Three Jewels for help in the attainment of liberation or Buddhahood.

GRASPING AT SELF-EXISTENCE *(bdag-'dzin).* The belief that oneself and phenomena are independently self-existent.

GREAT FACILITY *(shin-sbyangs; prasrabdha).* Great proficiency in focusing the consciousness on any object and remaining undistracted by the body which has become light and perfectly balanced.

GREAT SECRET VEHICLE *(gsang-chen theg-pa).* Synonyms: Vajra vehicle, Tantra vehicle.

GREAT VEHICLE *(theg-chen; mahayana).* The vehicle of Bodhisattvas. The goal of this vehicle is Buddhahood.

GURU *(bla-ma; guru).* See SPIRITUAL MASTER.

HAPPY BEING *(bde-'gro)*. Humans, demigods and gods are all known as happy beings because, although they lack true happiness, the three upper realms in which they live are extremely pleasant compared to the three unfortunate realms.

HEARKENERS *(nyan-thos; sravaka)*. Buddhists who have heard the Buddha's teachings but are able to engage only in the practises of the small vehicle. They have entered the paths of a hearkener which lead to solitary liberation and look primarily to the Sangha for assistance.

HEROES *(dpa'-bo, daka)*. A type of god that helps Tantric practitioners. Some live in cyclic existence, some in pure realms. In the field of the accumulation of merit they are emanations of Buddha.

HIGH REBIRTH *(mngon-mthos)*. Rebirth as a human, demigod or god. Synonym: happy rebirth.

HINDRANCES *(bar-gcod)*. See OUTER HINDRANCES, INNER HINDRANCES.

HOLDER OF THE VAJRA *(rdo-rje-'chang; Vajradhara)*.

INDEPENDENTLY SELF-EXISTENT *(rang-gi ngo-bos grub-pa)*. Synonyms: intrinsically existent, self-existent, truly existent.

INNER HINDRANCES *(nang-bar-bcod)*. Conditions unfavorable to Dharma practise such as the various mental afflictions, physical illnesses, etc.

INSPIRING STRENGTH *(byin-gyis brlab-pa; adhisthana)*. The power and influence of the objects of refuge that help to increase one's abilities and realizations.

INSTRUCTIONS OF GOING FOR REFUGE *(skyabs-'gro'i bslab-bya)*. The rules one must follow after taking refuge in the Three Jewels.

INTERMEDIATE STATE *(bar-do)*. The state between death and rebirth.

INTRINSICALLY EXISTENT (rang-bzhin-yod). See INDEPENDENTLY SELF-EXISTENT.

'JAM DPAL ZHAL LUNG *('jam-spal zhal-lung)*. A text on the stages of the path written by the Fifth Dalai Lama.

JAYULWA *(bya-yul-ba)*. A renowned Tibetan teacher in the Kadam lineage.

JE TSONG KHAPA *(rJe Tsong-kha-pa blo-bzang grags-pa)*. A great Tibetan guru from whom the Gelugpa lineage stems (1357-1419). See GANDEN KADAM LINEAGE.

JOR CH'O' *(sbyor-chos)*. The Lam Rim Puja compiled by Dagpo Losang Jampal Lhundrup.

KADAM LINEAGE *(bka'-gdams-brgyud)*. Literally, the lineage that gives instruction on Buddha's speech. This lineage, stemming from Atisha, holds the teachings of the three major lineages.

KARMA *(las; karma).* See DEEDS.

KAUSIKAH *(brgya-byin; Kaus'ika).* An epithet of Indra; a god in cyclic existence.

LATENCY *(bag-chags).*

LAZINESS *(le-lo).* Lack of enthusiasm and perseverance in the practise of virtue.

LEISURE *(dal-ba).* There are eight factors of leisure that allow one to practise Dharma. They are the freedom from birth: (1) as a hell being, (2) as a hungry ghost, (3) as an animal, (4) as a god, (5) as a person holding deluded views, (6) in a land without Dharma, (7) in a period when the Buddha or his representative is not present, (8) as a person who is demented or dumb.

LETHARGY *(rmugs).*

LIBERATION *(thar-pa).* See TRANSCENDENCE.

LINEAGE GURUS *(brgyud-pa'i bla-ma).* The lineage gurus are the unbroken succession of gurus from Buddha to the present through which the authoritative teachings and empowerments have been passed down.

LINEAGE OF THE PROFOUND VIEW *(zab-mo lta-brgyud).* The authoritative teachings on wisdom were passed down from Buddha Shakyamuni through Manjushri to an unbroken succession of gurus including Nagarjuna, Chandrakirti, Atisha, Je Tsong Khapa, etc.

LINEAGE OF VAST BODHISATTVA CONDUCT *(rgya-chen spyod-brgyud).* The authoritative teachings on Bodhisattva mind and activity were passed down from Buddha Shakya-muni through Maitreya to an unbroken succession of gurus including Asanga, Serlingpa, Atisha, Je Tsong Khapa, etc.

LINEAGE THAT BESTOWS THE INSPIRING STRENGTH OF TANTRIC PRACTISE *(nyams-len byin-rlabs bla-ma'i tsogs).* The teachings and empowerments of Tantric practise were passed down from Buddha Vajradhara through unbroken successions of masters.

LORD OF BIRDS *('dab-bzang gtzo-bo).* An epithet of the garuda.

LORD OF DEATH *('chi-bdag; yama).* See note no. 28.

LORD OF SAGES *(thub-pa'i dbang-po).* An epithet of Buddha. See BUDDHA.

MANDALA OFFERING *(mandala-dbul).* See note no. 13.

MARKS OF PERFECTION *(mtsan-dpe).* The thirty-two major and eighty minor physical characteristics of Buddha.

MASTER TEACHER *(ston-pa)*. See BUDDHA.

MEDITATIVE COMPOSURE *(mnyam-par-'jog)*.

MEMORY *(dran-pa)*. See note no. 33.

MENTAL AFFLICTIONS *(nyon-mong; klesha)*. The contaminated mental functions which are obstacles to liberation and causes of suffering. They are listed differently according to the various schools. The root mental afflictions are: (1) ignorance, (2) desire—attachment, (3) anger, (4) pride, (5) doubt, and (6) wrong views.

MENTAL EQUILIBRIUM *(sems-snyoms)*. See EQUILIBRIUM.

MERIT *(bsod-nams; punya)*. Virtuous deeds.

MILAREPA *(Mi-la-ras-pa)*. A renowned Tibetan practitioner of Dharma. Chief disciple of Marpa (1040-1123).

MINDFULNESS *(bag-yod)*. See note no. 33.

MORAL DOWNFALLS *(ltung-ba)*. Moral downfalls are deeds which cause rebirth in lower realms (thus, "downfalls"). These include the natural and proscribed non-virtuous deeds. Usually used in the compound "erroneous deeds and moral downfalls" (nyes-ltung).

MOUNT MERU *(lhun-po)*. Centre of the world as visualized in the mandala offering.

NAROPA *(Na-ro-pa)*. A renowned Indian pandit and practitioner of Dharma. Chief disciple of Tilopa and guru of Marpa.

NATURAL AND PROSCRIBED NON-VIRTUOUS DEEDS *(bcas-rang kha-na-ma tho'i las)*. See NATURAL NON-VIRTUES, PROSCRIBED NON-VIRTUES.

NATURAL NON-VIRTUES *(rang-bzhin kha-na-ma-tho-ba)*. Deeds associated with the mental afflictions; e.g., the ten non-virtuous actions which are: killing, stealing, sexual misconduct, false speech, harsh speech, slander, gossip, covetousness, malice, and wrong views. Synonyms: non-virtue, non-virtuous deeds, erroneous deeds, evil deeds.

NIHILISM *(chad-pa'i lta-ba)*. The false view that believes in the utter non-existence of all phenomena. This view is sometimes held by those who have misunderstood the teaching that phenomena are non-self-existent.

NON-SELF-EXISTENCE *(bdag-med-pa)*. Synonym of self-existencelessness. See ABSOLUTE TRUTH.

NON-VIRTUE *(mi-dge-ba)*. See NATURAL NON-VIRTUES.

NOT TRULY EXISTENT *(bden-med)*. See ABSOLUTE TRUTH, note no. 67.

OBEISANCE *(phag-'tsal-ba)*. Three types: obeisance of body which includes various types of prostrations, obeisance of speech which includes homage and praise, and obeisance of mind which includes reverence, respect, etc.

OBFUSCATIONS *(rnam-rtog)*. Obstacles to deep concentration.

OBJECTS OF REFUGE *(skyabs-yul)*. The Buddhist objects of refuge are the Three Jewels.

OBJECT TO BE REFUTED *(dgag-bye)*. See note no. 66.

OBSTRUCTIONS *(sgrib-pa; avarana)*. See TWO OBSTRUCTIONS.

OBSTRUCTIONS OF MENTAL AFFLICTIONS *(nyon-sgrib; klesha- varana)*. Obstacles to the attainment of liberation.

OBSTRUCTIONS TO OMNISCIENCE *(shes-sgrib; jneyavarana)*. Obstacles to the attainment of Buddhahood.

OMNISCIENT ONE *(kun-mkhyen)*. An epithet of Buddha. See BUDDHA.

ONE THOUSAND WORLD LEADERS *(zhing-gi 'dren-pa stong)*. The Buddhas who come to this world as world teachers during this eon.

ONE WHO HAS GONE TO SUCHNESS *(de-bzhin gshegs-pa; Tathagata)*. An epithet of Buddha. See BUDDHA.

OPENING THE DOOR TO THE SUPREME PATH *(lam-mchog sgo-'byed)*. The section of requests in Jor Cho *(the Lam Rim Puja)*.

ORAL INSTRUCTIONS *(man-ngag)*. Traditional explanations and instructions passed down orally through an unbroken lineage.

OUTER HINDRANCES *(phyi-bar-bcod)*. Conditions unfavorable to Dharma practise such as lack of nourishing food, poor shelter, etc.

PERFECT SERENE CONCENTRATION *(zhi-gnas-ting-'dzin)*.

PERFECT SERENITY *(zhi-gnas; samatha)*.

PHYSICAL ELEMENTS. See FOUR ELEMENTS.

POST MEDITATION *(rjes-thob)*.

PRECIOUS SUPREME DHARMA *(chos-dkon-mchog; dharma- ratna)*. Whatever is included in either the exalted truth of path or the exalted truth of cessation. In a nominal sense, this includes the authoritative teachings.

PROSCRIBED NON-VIRTUES *(bcas-pa'i kha-na-ma-tho-ba)*. Breaking of the precepts made by Buddha which one has vowed to keep.

PURE REALMS *(dag-pa'i zhing)*. Realms outside of cyclic existence where Buddhas, Bodhisattvas and practitioners with sufficient merit dwell.

PURIFYING FORCES *(dag-byed rkyen)*. See note no. 8. Synonym: four forces.

REALIZATIONS *(rtogs)*. Primarily refers to accomplishment in the three trainings.

RELATIVE TRUTH *(kun-rdzob bden-pa)*. Conventional existence; the interdependent existence of phenomena.

RELIGIOUS DRAMA *(gar)*. A drama depicting religious figures, deities, etc.

RENUNCIATION *(nges-'byung)*. To no longer desire the pleasures of cyclic existence.

ROOT GURU(S) *(rtza-ba'i bla-ma)*. One's main spiritual master(s) of this life.

SAKYA PANCHEN *(Sa-kya pan-chen)*. The renowned Tibetan guru, Sa-skya pandita Kun-dga'-rgyal-mtshan (1182-1251).

SAMSARA. See CYCLIC EXISTENCE.

SANGHA *(dge-'dun)*. See EXALTED SANGHA.

SCANNING MEDITATION *(shar-sgom)*. A series of contemplations and/or visualizations in sequence.

SELF-EXISTENT *(ngos-bos grub-pa)*. See INDEPENDENTLY SELF-EXISTENT.

SELF-EXISTENCELESSNESS *(bdag-med-pa)*. See ABSOLUTE TRUTH.

SEVEN LIMBS *(yan-lag-bdun)*. Obeisance, offerings, confession, rejoicing in virtue, requesting teachings, beseeching the gurus to live long, dedication of merit.

SEVEN SUPREME TREASURES OF A RULER OF MEN *(mi-dbang nor-mchog rin-chen rnam-pa-'dun)*. Precious wheel, precious jewel, precious queen, precious minister, precious elephant, precious horse, precious general.

SHIVA *(dbang-phyug; Isvara)*. A god in cyclic existence.

SINGLE-POINTED CONCENTRATION *(rtze-gcig gnas-pa'i ting-'dzin)*. Fixed concentration focused single-pointedly on an object. A stage in the development of perfect serenity.

SIX PERFECTIONS *(phyin-drug)*. Six practises of a Bodhisattva which lead to Buddhahood. The six are: giving, morality, patience, effort, deep concentration and wisdom.

SIX REALMS *(rigs-drug-gnas)*. The realms of the hell beings, hungry ghosts, animals, humans, demigods and gods.

SIX SPECIAL ELEMENTS *(sgos-khams-drug)*. The six elements (other than the four physical elements) which are necessary to practise Tantra.

SIX TYPES OF BEINGS *(rigs-drug)*. Hell beings, hungry ghosts, animals, humans, demigods and gods.

SMALL VEHICLE *(theg-dman; hinayana).* The vehicle of hearkeners and solitary victors. The goal of this vehicle is solitary liberation.

SOLITARY PEACE *(rang-nyid zhi-ba).* State of an arhat of the small vehicle—free of cyclic existence but without the attainment of Buddhahood. Synonyms: solitary liberation, solitary transcendence.

SOLITARY VICTORS *(rang-rgyal; pratyeka).* Buddhists who enter the paths of a solitary victor with the goal of solitary liberation. They rely mainly on the refuge of Dharma.

SPHERE OF DHARMA *(chos-dbyings; dharmdhatu).* See ABSOLUTE TRUTH.

SPIRITUAL GUIDE *(dge-ba'i bshes-gnyen; kalyanamitra or just bshes-gnyen).* See SPIRITUAL MASTER.

SPIRITUAL MASTER *(bla-ma; guru).* See note no. 16 for the qualifications of a spiritual master. Synonyms: guru, spiritual guide, spiritual protector.

SPIRITUAL MASTER—LORD OF THE SAGES—HOLDER OF THE VAJRA *(bla-ma thub-dbang rdo-rje-'chang).* The composite central figure in the field of the accumulation of merit. See note no. 3.

SPIRITUAL PROTECTOR *(yongs-'dzin).* Literally, completely holding (one from falling into unfortunate states). The outer Spiritual Protector is one's Spiritual Master. The inner Spiritual Protector is one's own wisdom. See SPIRITUAL MASTER.

SPIRITUAL SON *(sras, or rgyal-sras; Jinaputra).* Literally, "Son of the Victorious One" or "Prince". Synonym: Bodhisattva.

STAGES OF THE BODHI PATH *(byang-chub lam-gyi rim-pa).* The levels of practise leading to bodhi. See note no. 21.

STATE OF UNIFICATION *(zung-'jug).* The Tantric term for Buddhahood.

SUBLIME OFFERINGS *(kun-bzang mchod-sprin).* Offerings of the Bodhisattva Samantabhadra or offerings similar to them.

SUFFERING OF CHANGE *('gyur-ba'i sdug-bsngal).* One of the three sufferings. See note no. 49.

SUFFERING OF CONDITIONAL EXISTENCE *('du-byed-kyi sdug-bsngal).* One of the three sufferings. See note no. 46.

SUFFERING OF MISERY *(sdug-bsngal-gyi sdug-bsngal).* One of the three sufferings. See note no. 49.

SUPREME VEHICLE *(theg-mchog).* Synonym: great vehicle.

SUTRA *(mdo, sutra).* The discourses of Buddha.

TAKING REFUGE. Synonym: going for refuge.

TANTRA *(rgyud, or sngags).* The secret teachings and practises.

THREE BASKETS *(sde-snod-gsum; Tri-pitaka)*. Buddha's teachings of Sutra (discourses), Vinaya (discipline), and Abhi-dharma (metaphysics).

THREE BODIES *(sku-gsum)*. (1) The body of physical manifestation, (2) the body of utility, and (3) the body of Dharma which includes the body of Dharma knowledge and the Body of Dharma nature.

THREE DELIGHTS *(mnyes-pa-gsum)*. The three ways to please the guru.

THREE DOORS *(sgo-gsum)*. Body, speech and mind.

THREE JEWELS *(dkon-mchog-gsum)*. Buddha, Dharma and Sangha.

THREE LEVELS *(sa-gsum)*. On, below and above the earth.

THREE LINEAGES *(brgyud-pa gsum)*. The lineage of vast Bodhisattva conduct, the lineage of profound view, and the lineage that bestows the inspiring strength of Tantric practise.

THREE PLACES OF EXISTENCE *(srid-gsum)*. On, below and above the earth.

THREE REALMS *(khams-gsum)*. Desire, form and formless realms. The desire realm includes hell beings, hungry ghosts, animals, humans, demi-gods, and desire realm gods. The form realm includes form realm gods, and the formless realm includes the formless realm gods.

THREE SECRETS *(gsang-gsum)*. Vajra body, speech and mind.

THREE SUFFERINGS *(sdug-bsngal-gsum)*. Misery, change and conditional existence. See note no. 49.

THREE TIMES *(dus-gsum)*. Past, present and future.

THREE TRAININGS *(bslab-gsum; trisiksa)*: (1) Extraordinary morality, (2) extraordinary concentration, (3) extraordinary wisdom. These three trainings are extraordinary because they are based upon the practise of going for refuge to the Three Jewels.

THREE TYPES OF FAITH *(dad-pa-gsum)*: "faith" in Tibetan means clarity of mind. It should not be confused with "blind faith." There are three main types of true faith: admiration, aspiration and conviction See note no. 32.

THREE TYPES OF VOWS *(sdom-gsum)*. The vows of individual liberation, the Bodhisattva vows and the Tantric vows.

TIME OF DEGENERATION *(snyigs-dus)*. The present time period has five degenerations. See FIVE DEGENERATIONS.

TIME OF LIGHT *(dus-spron-me)*. The second half of an eon during which the average lifespan of beings is decreasing. This time of increasing unhappiness is conducive to the practise of Dharma and so Buddhas appear as world teachers. Thus it is known as a time of light.

TRANSCENDENCE *(mya-ngna-las 'das-pa, or 'das, nirvana)*. Literally, transcendence of sorrow. This is a general term which may refer to the state of a Buddha (see Buddhahood) or to the states of small vehicle arhats (see SOLITARY PEACE).

TRANSCENDENTAL WISDOM *(sher-phyin; prajnaparamita)*. This term may refer to three things: (1) the transcendental wisdom sutras, (2) the direct perception of voidness, or (3) resultant transcendental wisdom which is the omniscience of Buddhahood.

TRUE NATURE *(gnas-lugs)*. See ABSOLUTE TRUTH.

TUSHITA *(dga'-ldan; Tusita)*. Pure realm of the next world teacher, Maitreya.

TWO ACCUMULATIONS *(tsogs-gnyis)*. Merit and wisdom.

TWO BENEFITS *(don-gnyis)*. See ULTIMATE BENEFIT FOR SELF AND OTHERS.

TWO HIGHER REALMS *(khams gong-ma-gnyis)*. The form and formless realms.

TWO OBSTRUCTIONS *(skyon-sgrib-gnyis)*. (1) The obstructions of mental afflictions, and (2) the obstructions to omniscience.

TWO STAGES (OF TANTRA) *(rim-gnyis)*. The developing stage and the fulfilment stage.

TWO SUPREME BODIES *(mchog-sku-gnyis)*. (1) The body of form which includes the body of utility and the body of physical manifestation; and (2) the body of Dharma, which includes the Body of Dharma knowledge and the body of Dharma nature.

TWO TYPES OF ARHATSHIP *(dgra-bcom-rnam-gnyis)*. (1) The solitary liberation of a hearkener and (2) of a solitary victor. See ARHAT.

ULTIMATE BENEFIT FOR SELF AND OTHERS *(rang-gzhan don-gnyis mthar-phyin)*. The state of Buddhahood, which possesses the qualities of complete cessation and knowledge, compassion etc. Synonyms: dual goal, two benefits.

UNFORTUNATE REALMS *(ngan-song)*. The realms of hell beings, hungry ghosts and animals.

UNIFICATION. See STATE OF UNIFICATION.

UNQUIET *('du-'dzi)*. External or internal distractions.

UPPER REALMS *(mtho-ris)*. The realms of humans, demigods and gods. Synonyms: happy realms, fortunate realms.

UTTERLY NON-EXISTENT *(gtan-med)*. Non-existent in every sense, including the conventional sense.

VAJRA MASTER *(rdo-rje slob-dpon)*. Synonym: Tantric master.

VAJRA VEHICLE *(rdo-rje theg-pa; Vajrayana)*. Synonyms: vehicle of Tantra, great secret vehicle.

VENERABLE MEDICINE BUDDHA *(rje-sman-pa'i rgyal-po)*. One of the eight Medicine Buddhas.

VICTORIOUS ONE *(rgyal-ba; jina)*. An epithet of Buddha. See BUDDHA.

VISHNU *(khyab-'jug; Vishnu)*. A god in cyclic existence.

VOIDNESS *(stong-ba-nyid; sunyata)*. See ABSOLUTE TRUTH and note no. 67.

VOID OF SELF-EXISTENCE *(ngo-bos-stong-pa)*. See ABSOLUTE TRUTH and note no. 67.

VOWS *(sdom-pa)*. A commitment to keep any of the various types of precepts established by Buddha. See THREE TYPES OF VOWS.

VOWS OF INDIVIDUAL LIBERATION *(so-sor thar-pa'i sdom-pa or so-sor thar-pa; pratimoksa)*. The precepts established by Buddha Shakyamuni for Buddhist laymen, monks and nuns.

WATER POSSESSING EIGHT QUALITIES *(yan-lag brgyad-ldan-chu)*. Cool, clear, tasty, soft, light, odorless, harmless to the throat, and harmless to the stomach.

WORLD RULER *('khor-sgyur; Cakravartin)*.

YAMA *(gshin-rje; yama)*. See LORD OF DEATH.

YON TAN GZHI GYUR MA *(Yon-tan gzhi-gyur-ma)*. A short segment from Jor Cho which gives the essential points of the entire path very concisely.